THE GOSPELS,
PORTRAITS OF CHRIST

THE GOSPELS
PORTRAITS OF CHRIST

by

Wayne G. Rollins

THE WESTMINSTER PRESS
Philadelphia

LIBRARY OF CONGRESS CATALOG CARD No. 64–10044

PUBLISHED BY THE WESTMINSTER PRESS ®

PHILADELPHIA 7, PENNSYLVANIA

PRINTED IN THE UNITED STATES OF AMERICA

To Donnalou

CONTENTS

PREFACE

Imagine a Syrian Orthodox scribe, an Italian civil service employee, a British man of letters, and a Franciscan monk writing simultaneously on a common subject of mutually immense significance, and you have approximated the differences that characterize the four Gospels. The dividing lines among Matthew, Mark, Luke, and John are not so much a product of intention as of inevitability; each is a unique creature, writing in his own corner of the world, addressing a special culture in a unique historical situation. Even though a substantial block of common tradition is employed by each, the Gospel makers cannot help speaking in the forms and patterns that seem most compatible to their own religious and intellectual rhythms.

The present volume is concerned to explore the uniqueness that marks each of the Gospels. Although the special geographical, chronological, and professional characteristics of the four are important and obvious marks of their identity, emphasis will be placed on the intellectual, or what might be called "perspectual," differences among them: how each symbolizes God and his relation to the cosmos; how each characterizes human nature; how each diagnoses the essentials of Christian living; how each rehearses in name, story, and title the significance of Jesus for the human situation.

The method employed in piecing together these portraits

9

by the Gospel writers is discussed in the first chapter, " The New Approach." The next four chapters illustrate the method in motion in each of the four Gospels. And a brief postscript suggests the implications of the method and of the resultant portraits for present-day Christians as they " proclaim " their own inevitably unique renditions of the " good news " in their own habitats.

Some of the data and conclusions represented here are new; many are inherited from a succession of New Testament scholars ranging from the early 1920's to the present; and most of them have been worked over in a series of New Testament seminars on the Christology of the Synoptics, at Wellesley College from 1959 to 1962. Though the students are too numerous to mention, they have all left their mark on the observations and conclusions cited here.

Grants from the Hans W. Huber Foundation and the Wellesley College faculty research fund are gratefully acknowledged. Special thanks are due my wife, Donnalou, who entertained children, a siege of measles, and the typing of this manuscript simultaneously.

W. G. R.

Wellesley, Massachusetts

I THE NEW APPROACH

As a result of a two-party theological system dominating the religious scene twenty to fifty years ago, most Americans have been subjected to one of two misleading portraits of the Gospels: either the static one, propagated by fundamentalism, or the romantic one, developed by liberalism.

Within the past forty years, however, the Gospels have been approached in a new way. The new method might well be called " the approach of dynamic realism " — " dynamic " because it interprets the Gospels as products of complex and interacting religious, intellectual, and cultural forces; " realistic " because it regards the Gospels first and foremost as ancient documents to be approached with historic and linguistic care if one wishes to discover their *original* purpose and meaning.

PEELING THE ONION

The new approach is actually the result of spadework done in the early 1800's. Since that time New Testament scholarship has taken giant steps in recapturing the dynamic biography of the Gospels. Under the banner of three fresh disciplines — textual criticism, source criticism, and form criticism — scholars have developed a life portrait of the

11

Gospels that compares pictorially with the life story of an onion, which attains full-blown maturity through layer upon layer of progressively younger parts of itself.

1. In terms of this image, the " Christ event " constitutes the *core* of the Gospels. It consists of all those original but now obscure elements, such as the teachings, acts, death, and resurrection of Jesus, which we can no longer experience firsthand but must perforce examine through the eyes of " secondhand " witnesses.

2. *Oral circulation* of isolated sayings and stories constitutes the first stage in the gradual expansion from the core. Certainly most of the major events in Jesus' life were recorded, not on the spot, but on the basis of later reflection. In view of the fact that illiteracy prevailed among the masses in the first-century world, that most of the " people of the earth " who followed Jesus probably relied on memory more than on the written word, and that writing materials were scarce, we have every reason to conclude that Jesus' sayings, stories, and parables were first circulated in much the same way that news travels today until it becomes publicly newsworthy — by word of mouth. Like Mary, the early followers of Jesus kept these things in their hearts (Luke 2:51) until a historian like Luke solicited their ponderings for publication and dissemination among the Christian community at large (ch. 1:1-4).

3. However, before the Gospel writers edited the materials, another stratum of development intervened, namely, the *creation of small collections* in either oral or written form. The Beatitudes (Matt. 5:1-12) probably constitute an example. The reason for such collections was the growing needs that were generating in the lives of the primitive Christian communities as they expanded their operations to include regular worship services, preaching to the growing ranks of

the curious and providing instruction for recent converts and the young.

Various collections were useful for special purposes. For example, collections of *sayings* could be used in teaching or preaching. *Paradigms* or *pronouncement stories* (a narrative with a moral tacked to the end, such as Mark 2:27-28, " The sabbath was made for man, not man for the sabbath; so the Son of man is lord even of the sabbath ") were advantageously employed in controversy, in this particular instance to defend a Sunday versus a Saturday sabbath. Collections of *miracle stories* and *legends* such as the birth stories were used as window dressing to attract new members as well as to express the faith of the old. The *Passion narrative,* regarded by Rudolf Bultmann as the earliest literary composition of the church, was useful for a variety of purposes: it could be used for apologetics, explaining why Jesus was crucified even though avowedly blameless; it could be employed in preaching and exhortation to encourage and inspire those who might have to suffer a similar death; or it could be used in *worship* to commemorate and expound the significance of his death. One of the uses of the *genealogical* collections (Luke, ch. 3, and Matt., ch. 1) was to provide Jesus with a pedigree that would silence those who contested his Messianic lineage from David.

Naturally, different collections were developing in different centers of Christianity. We have reason to believe that the " Peter tradition " was circulating in Rome, the " John tradition " in Ephesus, et cetera. In fact, a recent archaeological discovery provides evidence that a special collection and theological tradition were developing in Egypt between the first and fourth centuries. In *The Secret Sayings of Jesus,* Robert M. Grant [1] provides commentary and translation of a collection unearthed in an Egyptian village in 1945. The collection, named The Gospel of Thomas, includes sayings both familiar and unfamiliar to our Gospels; for example, saying No. 32, " Jesus said: No prophet is acceptable in his village; no physician heals those who know him "; and saying No. 43, " Jesus said: Come into being as you pass away." On the basis of this evidence and on sheer historical probability, it seems likely that some of the sayings of Jesus may still lie buried in collections that never happened to come to light at the time the Gospels were being written between A.D. 65 and 100.

4. The next stage is the *composition of the Gospels* themselves. In all probability this took place under the sponsorship of an earlier version of the Ford or the Rockefeller Foundation. The Gospel authors were not just free-lance writers; they were hired or appointed by communities — Mark in Rome, Luke somewhere in Greece, Matthew in Antioch (?), John in Ephesus (?) — to weave the fragments and collections of oral and written tradition into a pattern suitable to their tastes and those of the sponsors.

But why were these Gospels commissioned at all? Why weren't the communities satisfied with the free-floating collections they already had? The explanation seems to involve three different motives. First, the imminent end of the cosmos which had been anticipated for so long never developed. While hopes were still high that the Son of Man would come on the clouds of heaven any day, only temporary provision was needed for the spiritual and ecclesiastical life of the community. However, as more and more Christians succumbed, skepticism over the imminence of the Second Coming increased. Eyes turned away from outer space and back to earth. Consequently, a haphazard collection of reminiscences and sayings would not suffice; a longer, more substantial, and more comprehensive collection was demanded.

A second motivation for commissioning the Gospels was

the necessity of collecting and recording as many as possible
of the recollections and remembered sayings of Jesus from
the original eyewitnesses before they died. Peter, it is ru-
mored, died about A.D. 64. James the brother of John and
son of Zebedee had been executed by Herod Agrippa in A.D.
44 (Acts 12:2). James the brother of Jesus was reportedly
stoned to death in A.D. 62. Before the tradition dissolved in
the hands and faulty memories of secondhand recipients it
was necessary to stabilize it in some form.

A third reason was the increase of theological splinter
groups. Disagreement and division, eventually to be defined
as heresy, necessitated an authoritative document to adjudi-
cate differences.

So the Gospels were composed. Have we any indication of
the sources they employed? Did they borrow from one another? Which collections did they depend upon? *Source
criticism* seeks to answer these questions. B. H. Streeter, the
patron saint of the source critics, enumerates his findings in
the classic volume *The Four Gospels*.[2] A paraphrase of
Streeter's conclusions includes the following:

1. Both Matthew and Luke use Mark as one of their sources,
Matthew employing most of Mark (600 out of Mark's 661 verses),
Luke using only one half (350 of Mark's 661 verses).

2. Mark's sources are indeterminate, beyond the near certainty
that he employed oral and written collections. Papias, a second-
century Christian, proposes that one of Mark's sources was the
apostle Peter, who, Papias maintains, instructed Mark personally.

3. Matthew and Luke share another body of material that is
totally absent from Mark. The Germans have given this source
the name of Q (for *Quelle* = " source "). Whether Q is oral, written, or a mixture of the two is uncertain. Q includes such passages
as the long version of the temptation story (Matt. 4:1-11; Luke
4:1-13), the Lord's Prayer (Matt. 6:9-13; Luke 11:2-4), and
the parable of the leaven (Matt. 13:33; Luke 13:20-21).

4. Matthew also employs special material designated as M or
" Special-Matthew," which includes, among other elements, the

story of the Wise Men (ch. 2:1-12) and the parable of the ten virgins (ch. 25:1-13).

5. Luke also admits of original material called L. Examples are the parable of the prodigal son (ch. 15:11-32), the parable of the good Samaritan (ch. 10:29-37), and the " road to Emmaus " story (ch. 24:13-27).

Streeter's theory is widely accepted by New Testament scholars today, including a growing edge of prominent Roman Catholic Bible critics.

5. The present portrait of the Gospel " onion " would not be complete without reference to a fifth important stage, namely, *Gospel copy-making*. Neither we, nor Matthew, nor Luke know the Gospel of Mark in the original. All of us have to rely on copies. The copies used by Matthew and Luke were secondhand. Ours are at least twentieth-hand, and for most of us, in translation. The Biblical statement, " The spirit indeed is willing, but the flesh is weak," describes the copyist's predicament quite well. On the basis of the Greek manuscript copies of the New Testament available to us — more than a thousand — it appears that no scribe, regardless of how zealous, conscientious, or dedicated, was able to avoid making copying errors.

Textual criticism makes its business the task of studying the errors and disagreements among the manuscripts, and the more formidable task of deciding which reading among several dissident readings is most likely to be the original. For example, Luke 11:2, the first line of the Lord's Prayer, is rendered in two different ways in the available manuscript copies of this prayer. Some manuscripts simply read, " Father, hallowed be thy name." Others read, " Our Father who art in heaven, hallowed be thy name." Which did Luke really write and which copy is the mistaken one? The textual critic answers, " The first is the original, for two reasons." The shorter reading is more likely authentic than the longer one on the basis of the contention that the copyists were more apt to add than to subtract from holy writ. They could justify what they added as helpful explanation, but under no circumstances could they defend a deletion.

Second, in this instance the *motivation* for the scribe's addition is transparent. His familiarity with the longer version of the Lord's Prayer as recorded *in Matthew* motivates him to expand Luke to match Matthew. Textual critics find the tendency to harmonize sayings in Matthew, Mark, and Luke rather common among copyists.

6. Stage six in the creation of our English Bible consists of *the translation process*. A complete translation of the New Testament in English first appeared in 1382, in the hand of John Wycliffe. However, long before Wycliffe the Gospels had been translated into Coptic, Syriac, Armenian, Latin, and Georgian — in fact, within four centuries of their composition. The platitude that " something is lost in translation " applies especially to a two-thousand-year-old document. The essential " something " lost in the translation of an ancient work is its original connotation. If a contemporary writer were to slip the phrases " new deal " or " new frontier " into a sentence, bells would ring for Democrat and Republican readers alike. However, the allusion would probably escape a reader twenty centuries from now unless he were well versed in the Roosevelt-Kennedy era. Likewise, were it not for New Testament historians and linguists who are well versed in the idiomatic quality of first-century Greek, much of the allusive and connotative power of New Testament phrases and words would escape the twentieth-century reader. An example is the Fourth Gospel's description of Jesus as " the Word " (Greek, *logos*). Unless the reader is familiar with the range of connotations that this

term carried for Platonic and Neoplatonic philosophy during the New Testament era, he can only guess at its original meaning.

Although they were compiled as the " church's books," a factor perhaps more important than any other in determining their final flavor is the editorial and compositional activity of the Gospel author.

THE ART OF THE GOSPEL MAKER

The Gospel maker is both an editor and an artist. As an *editor,* he marks the literature with his efforts at compiling and organizing the data into readable, usable form. As with any other editor, the style of his technique is quite visible. When we compare the editorial " fingerprints " of Matthew, Mark, Luke, and John we find certain standard differences developing among them.

1. *Geographical locales differ.* Although in Mark 11:25-26 the saying about forgiving " your " enemies so that " you " might be forgiven occurs in southern Palestine a few days before the crucifixion, the same saying is recorded in Matt. 6:14 in northern Palestine at the beginning of Jesus' ministry.

2. *Traditional material differs.* Luke's tradition tells the Gospel editor that Jesus' parents were residents of Nazareth who traveled to Bethlehem at the time of his birth only because a census had been required. Matthew's sources, however, suggest that Joseph and Mary lived in Bethlehem and were fleeing to Nazareth only to avoid the threat of Herod's son, Archelaus.

3. *The sequence of events differs.* A quick comparison of Mark and Luke, especially, will reveal this difference. Source critics have observed that although Luke follows Mark's wording quite carefully, he changes his order or sequence of

material. Matthew, on the other hand, follows Mark's order but freely revises his wording. Examples of this will be noted throughout the present volume.

4. *The clustering of stories and sayings differ.* A choice example is the Sermon on the Mount compared in Matthew and Luke. That which is a neat literary package in Matthew turns out to be a scattering of epigrams in Luke.

5. *The form of quotations differs.* Frequently an indirect quotation in Mark becomes a direct quotation in Matthew.

Matt. 12:10	Mark 3:1-2
And behold, there was a man with a withered hand. And they asked him, " Is it lawful to heal on the sabbath? " so that they might accuse him.	. . . and a man was there who had a withered hand. And they watched him, to see whether he would heal him on the sabbath, so that they might accuse him.

In general, Matthew and Luke tend to dress up Mark's simple, often awkward style by such measures.

6. *The length of narrative differs.* Both Matthew and Luke pare down Mark's rendition of the feeding of the five thousand (Mark 6:30-44; Matt. 14:13-21; Luke 9:10-17). Examples are numerous.

In addition to playing the role of editor, the Gospel maker is also an *artist*. This means that the portrait he paints reflects not only the character of the subject but the style and mind of the artist as well. In the colors he chooses, in his organization of materials, in his use of contrast and highlighting, the artist leaves traces of himself, the shape of his mind, the breadth of his vision, the range of his imagination, and even the quality of his art. It is not pure Jesus who appears in the Gospels, but Jesus-as-seen-through-the-eyes-of-Mark, or Matthew.

This fact presents a peculiar challenge to the modern New Testament reader who is concerned to understand the nature of the subject more than the artist. The challenge is that he must become more sophisticated than his literalist or romanticizing predecessors in approaching the Gospels. The old psychiatric joke about two clinicians passing in the hall, the one greeting, " Good morning. How are you? " and the other walking off muttering, " What did he mean by that? " applies here. To discover the intent of any man's words, it is necessary to know the man or to learn as much as possible about his state of mind, his prejudices, predilections, and the like. Only having done this, can we discover " what he meant by that." To know what Matthew, Mark, or Luke meant by his peculiar rendition of the Gospel narrative, we must first understand him, and then proceed to the task of defining for ourselves the line between history and interpretation, between the subject and the artist.

THE TASK AT HAND

Our immediate business is to study the four Evangelists in operation, to evaluate their skill as theologians, to observe the way they move through their material, and to note their idiosyncrasies. Of special interest in our study is the Gospel writer's Christology, how the peculiar bent of his mind echoes in the way he describes Jesus of Nazareth. Which Christological labels is he most apt to apply to Jesus? On which aspects of Jesus' life does he dwell? On teaching the crowds, healing the sick, his violent death, or the mysterious resurrection? Where does he locate Jesus' " saving power "? In his words of absolution, in the cosmic implications of his death, in his promise of the world to come, or in his challenge to follow him in the world as it is? The " laboratory " method in this investigation involves two principal procedures.

Comparative analysis. The weight of the argument will ride on a comparison of Matthew's, Mark's, Luke's, and John's treatment of common material. The reader can pursue this investigation independently by studying the *Gospel Parallels* (RSV),[3] a book in which the three texts of the Synoptic Gospels are printed side by side. One or two examples of this method will suffice. First, let us note how Matthew, Mark, and Luke render the parable about new and old wineskins. Each attaches his own twist to the account.

Matt. 9:17	Mark 2:22	Luke 5:39
. . . but new wine is put into fresh wineskins, and so both are preserved.	. . . but new wine is for fresh skins.	And no one after drinking old wine desires new; for he says, " The old is good."

Matthew's ending quite obviously argues that the old (the Old Testament and Jewish law) should not be discarded in favor of the new; the legalism of Judaism and the new law of Christ must be wed. Jesus has come not to destroy the law but to fulfill it (Matt. 5:17, an M passage!), a typical Matthean emphasis.

Mark's rendition evinces neither care nor contempt for the old. He concentrates on one thing, the presence of the new in Jesus, here and now, and its demand for new religious forms, untrammeled by the limitations of the past.

Luke maintains the goodness of the old because of his audience. Largely Greek, as Luke himself is, his audience regard Moses and Abraham as strangers and foreigners and therefore are indisposed to recognize the worth of the Old Testament. Yet Luke's purpose is to sell them on the importance of the Old Testament, because for Luke it is absolutely necessary to understand the Old Testament before one can become a Christian. The evidence for this thesis will be supplied later (though see Acts 8:34-40; Luke 24:44 ff.).

Synoptic comparisons yield a rich harvest of differences, from the subtle to the striking. The parable of the sower offers an example of a subtle difference. At the same spot in the narrative, the Evangelists decide to use their own term for the devil: Matthew uses " the evil one " (Matt. 13:19); Mark, " Satan " (Mark 4:15); and Luke, " the devil " (Luke 8:12). Are these variations intentional? If so, do they express mere preference or theological contention? The parable of the marriage feast, however, offers an example of striking difference. The two accounts are well worth puzzling over in detail. Here we need cite only the " moral " attached to each version as it appears in Matthew and Luke. Matthew reads: " For many are called, but few are chosen " (ch. 22:14), which reflects his pet thesis that among the elect, only the truly righteous will be chosen for eternal life. Luke's ending is, " For I tell you, none of those men who were invited shall taste my banquet " (ch. 14:24), reflecting the famous Lucan motif that the Jews (those declining the invitation) shall be displaced (not " taste my banquet ") by the conversion of the Gentiles, a thesis that caused Paul and the Jerusalem church no end of controversy.

Internal analysis is a second method of Synoptic comparison. This method consists of addressing each Gospel with a series of questions designed to detect possible differences. These questions relate particularly to the intellectual and theological idiosyncrasies of the Synoptic authors. What are his favorite words and special interests? How does he argue his case? By dramatic illustration, by accusation, or by formal argumentation? What is the locus of his appeal? The will, the mind, or the heart? These questions also relate to his religious orientation. How does he define sin? What does he conceive to be the " highest good "? What does he believe a man must do to be saved? These questions inquire into his audience. Are they Jewish or Gentile? Do they appear to be wealthy or poor? educated or uneducated?

With the use of these methods in the following four chapters, two major sets of theses will be developed. The first of these proposes that the Gospel makers approach reality from different directions. Mark's is described as a religious-existential approach; Matthew's, as ethical-apocalyptic; Luke's as aesthetic-historical; and John's, as paradoxical-mystical. The specific intention of the terms will subsequently be defined.

The second thesis holds that the real as opposed to the professed centers of the worlds of the Gospel writers are not identical. Mark's Gospel is clearly Christocentric. Matthew appears to be solidly anthropocentric, or " man-centered." Luke, the credulous and inventive Greek, is theocentric, or " God-centered." And John is Logos-centered, or word-centered, which in a contemporary idiom might be rendered, " God-man–centered."

II THE GOSPEL OF MARK:
A Religious-Existential Approach

One day not long ago, as I was leaving a café in Paris, I passed a group of students, one of whom stepped up to me and said: " Sûrement, Monsieur est existentialiste! "

I denied that I was an existentialist. Why? I had not stopped to consider, but doubtless I felt that terms suffixed by *ist* usually conceal vague generalities.

Jean Wahl opens *A Short History of Existentialism* [4] with this anecdote because, as a professional philosopher, he is even more wary than the layman of vague, general terms, particularly the term " existentialism." Sharing his wariness, we might well investigate this term before stamping it on the Gospel of Mark.

The Existential Question

Although we are not certain who first carved out the words " existential philosophy," most philosophers and practically all theologians trace the authorship of existentialism to the Danish journalist, philosopher, and theologian Søren Kierkegaard (1813–1855). Names that should be added to a modern list include the theologians Gabriel Marcel, Martin Buber, and Jacques Maritain; the German philosophers Karl Jaspers and Martin Heidegger; and the versatile French novelist, playwright, philosopher, and political activist Jean-

Paul Sartre. What makes them all existentialists? They are all existentialists because they ask a common question, namely, " Of what does existence, *my existence* and the existence of other men, consist? " To phrase the question more " existentially," " What does it mean personally for an individual to *exist* in this world as a thinking, loving, dying, hoping, working creature, caught between the anxiety of life's limitations and the aspiration toward freedom and self-expression? " " What meaning can be found in the life that every man lives between the desire to be an individual and the craving to share the lives of others, between the knowledge of death and the hope of immortality, between the security of rationality and the inspiration of conviction? " In brief, the existential question in the language of the existentialists is: " How can one achieve *authentic existence* between birth and death? " Perhaps it is really the same question the Philippian jailer addressed to Paul and Silas: " Men, what must I do to be saved? " (Acts 16:30).

An answer, which qualitatively resembles most existentialist positions, is proffered by Søren Kierkegaard: " The thing is to find a truth which is true for me, to find the idea for which I can live and die." As Calvin Schrag lucidly illustrates in *Existence and Freedom*,[5] the way to truth and to life for the existentialist is not the road of logical verification or empirical demonstration, though these techniques may play minor roles along the way. Basically the road is one of " passionate inwardness." The greatest truths, those which most seriously affect my existence, resist final attempts at verification. Whether this cause is more worthy than that, whether honor has greater value than self-preservation, whether mercy is preferable to sacrifice — all can be answered only by conscientious and courageous intuitive judgment.

Truth, for the existentialist, is analogous to faith. It is not something to which one intellectually subscribes but to which

one commits himself. It is verified not in being believed but
in being lived. Basic truth is always acclaimed with risk. We
cannot see with total clarity, yet we accept even though the
facts are not yet all in. Søren Kierkegaard defines faith as
" *objective uncertainty* held with an infinite *passion* of *inwardness.*"

" But how can anyone act with objective uncertainty? "
the essentialist asks. " You do it every day," the existentialist
answers. " Because we lack objective certitude does not imply we lack subjective certainty. Ninety-five percent of the
decisions we make daily are based either on good judgment,
common sense, or the hunch of experience."

The telling difference between the *essentialist* and the existentialist is that the former deals with part of man, qua
thinker, tabulator, investigator, and spectator; the latter
deals with more of this man, not only as one who thinks and
observes, but as one who participates actively in the world,
as one who loves, who hungers and thirsts both spiritually
and physically, and as one who eventually dies and is conscious of this before it happens.

The contrast is sharply illustrated in Kierkegaard's comment on the philosophy of the German essentialist, Friedrich
Hegel. Kierkegaard describes this kind of thinker as one who

erects an immense building, a system, a system which embraces
the whole of existence and world history, etc. — and if we con-
template his personal life, we discover to our astonishment this
terrible and ludicrous fact, that he himself personally does not live
in this immense high-vaulted palace, but in a barn alongside of it,
or in a dog kennel or at the most in the porter's lodge.[6]

What has all this to do with the Gospel of Mark? A modern existentialist theologian and Mark would probably be
able to break bread together congenially for a considerable
time, whereas Mark and Descartes or Hegel would not.

Many Marcan emphases echo the themes of modern existentialism: the emphasis on sensing the truth that lies deeper than mere sense perception, on understanding the meaning and significance of suffering and death, on striving after authentic existence by finding a truth worth living for, tolerating the objective uncertainty that often accompanies inward certitude, on seeking after authentic existence as a participant, not a spectator. This is not to say that Mark is an out-and-out existentialist; rather, that Mark's approach to reality shares significant features with the existentialist approach. Though terminologically foreign to one another, they bear remarkable psychological resemblance.

THE EXISTENTIAL CORE OF MARK

Mark is the Leonardo da Vinci of the Gospel writers. He has a sense for structure, contrast, and plot. He is a literary architect, dramatist, and perceptive theologian. In a sense he is also an inventor. The Gospel form, as far as we know, is his creation. In any event, his particular canvas provides the model for two others. Mark is the first to corral and muster the freely shifting elements of the " good news " into a defined literary shape; and as we shall have occasion to note later, the form is considerably sophisticated.

Mark, perhaps following Paul, put the word " gospel " in lights. Luke and John ignore the term entirely. Matthew employs it sparingly (chs. 4:23; 9:35; 24:14; 26:13). For Mark, however, the word " gospel " captures the breath and the fire of the Christ event. " Good news "! Not static, not confined to the printed word, but a slice of reality vitally related to every human being and his destiny. This is how Mark thinks of the gospel he proclaims.

As many lovers of Mark have noted, the structure into which he pours his good news is an architecturally superb specimen. The floor plan emerges from a focal center, namely, the crucial question Jesus addressed to his right-hand man, Peter, as they sat talking in the north country:

On the way he asked his disciples, "Who do men say that I am?" And they told him, "John the Baptist; and others say, Elijah; and others one of the prophets." And he asked them, "But who do you say that I am?" Peter answered him, "You are the Christ." And he charged them to tell no one about him. (Mark 8:27-30.)

This little interlude in the narrative exposes the nerve of the Marcan plot: Jesus' identity is a *mystery*.

The Identity of Jesus: An Objective Uncertainty. Mark's considerable contribution to New Testament Christology lies in his frankness about the historical Jesus in whom he perceives the power of God addressing him. Mark tries to communicate to his readers his own experience of hearing the story about Jesus for the first time. In all probability he was not sure at first who Jesus really was or whether he was what Peter or other followers of the Jesus cult acclaimed him to be. Mark surmises that for those who knew Jesus best, his family and his kinsmen, the identity of Jesus was objectively quite uncertain.

Mark communicates the truth and the importance of this fact in a variety of ways: in his treatment of the humanity of Jesus over against the treatments of Matthew and Luke; in his analysis and explanation of Jesus' silence about himself and his repression of any public confessions that he is the Christ or the Holy One of God, et cetera; and in his hints about the quality of Jesus' self-consciousness.

Mark's emphasis on the humanity of Jesus is disarming for some readers. Jesus frequently is made to appear and act like any other man. He is not the well-composed, omniscient figure portrayed in the Fourth Gospel. He shows anger at the Pharisees (Mark 3:5); he marvels at his kinsmen's unbelief (ch. 6:6); he sighs with spiritual fatigue when the Pharisees seek a sign (ch. 8:12); he looks with paternal love on the young man in search of eternal life, even after Jesus has given him the impossible assignment of selling all that he has to give to the poor (ch. 10:21).

Mark's reports on Jesus are so candid at times that Matthew and Luke choose to correct him for the benefit of the narrower public who may misinterpret or draw mistaken conclusions. More concerned with avoiding intellectual or theological embarrassment than with preserving history, they gouge a hole here or dab on a piece of putty there to make the Marcan picture presentable. A few details of the Marcan picture that show the tampering of a later hand will illustrate the point.

For example: (*a*) When Mark portrays Jesus as so fatigued that his friends have to retrieve him from the crowds, convinced that "he is beside himself" (Mark 3:19-21), Matthew and Luke choose to delete it. (*b*) Or when Mark frankly admits that Jesus has become so disillusioned with his fellow countrymen's skepticism that "he *could* do no mighty work there" (Mark 6:5), Matthew hastens to cover up the possible implication that Jesus' power was limited; he refines the passage with the slight word change, "he *did not* do many mighty works there" (Matt. 13:58), the clear implication being, he could have if he had wanted. (*c*) A similar cut in the script occurs in the statement found in Mark 9:37, somewhat disarming for cautious Christologists. Mark reads as follows: "Whoever receives one such child in my name receives me; and whoever receives me, receives *not me* but him who sent me." Matthew and Luke both see fit to perform surgery on the statement and remove the offensive " not me " from the body of the statement. (*d*) One of the most striking changes of Mark is found in Matt. 19:17. When Jesus *in Mark* asks the young man: "Why do you call me good? No one is good but God alone," Matthew's expurgated edition records: " Why do you ask me about what is good? One there is who is good." Matthew leaves the statement conveniently ambiguous. Where Mark leaves Jesus' identity in a state of objective uncertainty, Matthew and Luke frequently rush in with coddling revisions.

Another Marcan theme, that *Jesus suppresses information about himself,* also contributes to the objective uncertainty over Jesus' identification. This feature of Mark's Gospel was first described in considerable detail by Wilhelm Wrede in his work on " the Messianic secret " in Mark.[7]

Wrede's theory rests on this cornerstone: the author of the Gospel of Mark is concerned to explain to a querulous public why Jesus, if he was really the Son of God, was not recognized as such during his lifetime by more than a handful of people (Matthew, Luke, and John maintain that this is not the case at all). Mark's explanation is: " Jesus wanted it this way." To support this contention, Mark refers the reader to a number of instances in which Jesus consistently suppresses information about his true identity. For example, when he exorcizes a demon he commands the patient to keep silent about his benefactor (Mark 1:34; 3:12). He quells attempts to publicize his miracles (chs. 1:44; 5:43; 7:36; 8:26). He refuses to give " signs," to identify himself, with irrefutable evidence, to anyone of his generation (ch. 8:12), and he charges even his disciples to hush his identity until after his death (chs. 8:30; 9:9).

Mark, however, doesn't stop with this. Sharing the growing theological opinion of his day that God had hardened the hearts of the Jews (cf. Rom. 11:25), Mark repeats the party line with the theme that Jesus not only suppresses his identity but takes measures to mislead the opposition. For Mark, the purpose of the parable as a pedagogical device is not to enlighten but to keep the opposition in the dark, " so that they may indeed see but not perceive, and may indeed hear but not understand; *lest they should turn again, and be forgiven* " (Mark 4:12).

God also has had his hand in this concerted deception. He had hardened the hearts of the Jews (chs. 3:5; 7:6-7) and even of the disciples (chs. 6:52; 8:17). Mark makes no attempt to hide the fact that the disciples were blind to much that Jesus said and did during his lifetime (chs. 4:41; 5:31; 6:52; 9:28, 32). Their total defection at the crucial point of Jesus' life proves the instability of their commitment. They " all " forsook him and fled (ch. 14:23, 27, 29, 50), a point sharply made by Mark.

Granting that Jesus *may* have suppressed information about himself and granting that God *may* have hardened the hearts of men — a less credible assumption — why did they do it? Mark answers: if they had not, Jesus would not have been crucified. If Jesus had not been crucified, scripture would not have been fulfilled (ch. 14:49). If scripture had not been fulfilled, the will of God, his plan for human salvation, would not have developed as planned (v. 36).

What interests us in all this is not Mark's theological rationalization of the fact, but the fact itself, that Jesus' authority was not fully recognized or acclaimed until after the death and resurrection event.

The ambiguity in Jesus' self-consciousness as portrayed sketchily by Mark adds further fuel to the argument that Mark believes Jesus' identity before the crucifixion to have been objectively uncertain for his followers. Only once in Mark's Gospel does Jesus acquiesce to a title that comes to have theological importance in the later church. When the high priest asks whether he is the Christ, the Son of the Blessed, Jesus answers, " I am " (ch. 14:62). Aside from this one bold confession, of questionable historical value (though of dramatic and theological value to Mark), Jesus' statements about himself and his role are left ambiguous.

For instance, after Peter confesses that Jesus is "the Christ" (ch. 8:29), Jesus says neither yea nor nay. Only the Marcan formula follows: "And he charged them to tell no one about him." Does this mean that Jesus rejected the title of Christ (Hebrew, *māshīah*, "Messiah," "the anointed one" of David's line)? Not necessarily. But if we read on to Jesus' sharp rebuke of Peter, "Get behind me, Satan!" (v. 33), we discover another facet of Jesus' self-consciousness. Jesus' rebuke implies a vehement correction of Peter's illusion that Jesus will fulfill the Messianic image as popularly conceived, namely, as a new King of Jerusalem, but not as a sufferer at the hands of the people. "If you wish to call me the Messiah," Jesus is saying, "you will have to revise your image of Messiahship to include the possibility of suffering and death." Jesus' persistence in questioning the popular conception is seen also in ch. 12:35, where he dissociates the Messiah image from its popular, Davidic, militarist connotation.

Jesus persistently refuses to be labeled. He wishes his acts and deeds to be judged for themselves as the source of his authority. No other assurance of authority is possible (ch. 11:27-33).

Of all the Gospels, Mark alone presents Jesus' identity as *genuinely* problematic. Matthew and Luke repair this deficiency by supplying Jesus with all sorts of certifying proofs. His Davidic pedigree is secured by the genealogies; his divine origin, by the birth stories (Matt., chs. 1 and 2; Luke, chs. 1 and 2); his identity with the Father, by a fortuitous quotation (Matt. 11:25-27; Luke 10:21-22); his bona fide Lordship, by extended resurrection accounts which include phenomenal postresurrection encounters (Matt., ch. 28; Luke, ch. 24); whereas Mark closes his resurrection account without one phenomenal appearance of Jesus and with the women at the empty tomb in a state of puzzlement, amazement, fear, and objective uncertainty.

Jesus the Stranger. Mark, as opposed to Matthew and Luke, is a Christocentric Gospel. To be sure, Jesus is undeniably the *dramatic* center of all *three* Synoptic Gospels, but he is not the *real* center of each. By *real center,* we mean that he occupies the *real* attention of the author over against all other claims to attention, such as ethics, philosophies of history, and doctrines of God.

A careful perusal of the Gospels will bear this observation out, if one is willing on occasion to cross-examine the Gospel writers. A particularly useful question to address to each of the Gospel writers is what, in his estimation, one must do to be saved. The answers will not be the same for each. Matthew's answer would probably sound something like this: " Strive for the higher righteousness as revealed to you by God through the new law declared in Jesus." Luke's, like this: " Be instructed in the wonders of God's plan of salvation and then submit to baptism in order to receive the Spirit. Then go out and heal." But John's and Mark's would sound quite a bit alike. John's unadorned answer would probably be, " Believe in him whom he [God] has sent " (John 6:29). And Mark's terse, unelaborated answer would be, " Follow Jesus." For Matthew and Luke, the psychological or *real* centers are respectively ethics and theology of history. But for John and Mark, Jesus himself occupies their interest, their curiosity, and their religious concern.

Sherman Johnson, in his commentary on Mark,[8] appears to concur that Mark is radically Christocentric: " The theology of Mark is essentially a Christology." Mark does not care to speculate about the title that best fits Jesus' lapel; he is concerned with Jesus' function. " We are never told who he is," Johnson observes; " instead we see what happens when he appears."

What does happen when Jesus appears in Mark's Gospel? He is marveled at, acclaimed, accoladed, celebrated — but in the end, dealt with as a *stranger*.

When Albert Camus wrote his novel entitled *The Stranger,* he may well have been attempting to sketch a life of Christ — in the negative. Mersault, the stranger, is condemned to death for a capital offense for which he was not guilty. Camus makes clear that the reason for his indictment was the prejudicial attitude of the proper jury who sat in judgment upon him. When Mersault innocently and candidly confesses that he has not observed the pious, inane amenities which the jury feel are so important, they combine their indignation with circumstantial evidence to produce a verdict of " guilty."

In some respects the portrait of Jesus' fate in Mark provides a template for Camus's Mersault, though the specific gravities of the two differ greatly. Jesus is a *stranger* in Mark, even for those people into whose midst he has brought health. We read that " they began to beg Jesus to depart from their neighborhood " (ch. 5:17). He turned out to be more bizarre, more serious, and more demanding than they had anticipated in their original awe and curiosity. Because he is *the stranger,* Jesus suffers death at the hands of those who find his strangeness intolerable. The fact of Jesus' death becomes the monumental reality dominating Mark's Gospel.

The suffering and death of Jesus lay hold of Mark's mind. Although it had tragic dimensions, the death was overshadowed by an element of sublimity. For Mark, Jesus' death was a work of art, a masterpiece to be studied closely, to be examined in detail, to be devoutly treasured, and if necessary, to be emulated. Mark regards Jesus' death as premeditated, planned in advance (chs. 8:31; 9:31; 10:33), and executed with discipline and precision. " The Son of man . . . came not to be served but to serve, and to give his life as a ransom for many." (Ch. 10:45.) Mark implies Jesus intentionally set his face toward the gates of Jerusalem, despite the protestations of his disciples, to force this holy city into a decision. Will they accept or reject him? Will they acquit or indict him?

In crasser terms, Jesus performs an experiment in morality. He uses his life as the constant. Will the system be able to absorb his life into its habitual pattern? Will it be forced to adapt to a new pattern? Or will it be forced to make public declaration that a life like his and a system like theirs cannot coexist — one or the other must be destroyed? Only in offering his body as the vehicle of the experiment would he discover the answer for himself and for the citizenry of Jerusalem.

The death of Jesus taught Jerusalem something about itself that it was never quite able to forget. This was no mere accident. Mark tries to make clear that Jesus knew exactly what the risk was and what the cost would be. Jesus wanted one thing, to intrude his consciousness into the consciousness of the city, its shopkeepers, its militia, its priests, and its people. He wanted to force them out of their neutrality into a decision over his life and death.

Jesus took the risk. He made contact. At the point of his death a Roman centurion, far from home on an unpleasant assignment, moved out of the shadows of neutrality into an unsolicited appraisal: " Truly this man was a Son of God."

Sight and Insight. Isaiah of Jerusalem records his sense of mission in these words, in the form of a personal oracle from the Lord of Hosts (Isa. 6:9-10):

Go, and say to this people:
> "Hear and hear, but do not understand;
> see and see, but do not perceive."
> Make the heart of this people fat,
>> and their ears heavy,
>> and shut their eyes;
> lest they see with their eyes,
>> and hear with their ears,
> and understand with their hearts,
>> and turn and be healed.

Like defensive lovers, anxious to justify what they see in each other and why others fail to see it, the early church found in this passage from Isaiah an expression of their own experience. Mark adapts this theme from Isaiah to articulate the basic difference between men of faith and disbelievers. The former have eyes and see with them, the others have eyes but are blind.

No explanation of this historic opposition between the blind and the seers is offered. The fact is simply observed. Some men have learned to see through the facade of reality into its deeper meaning, others never go beyond a state of pedestrian vision. Is it impossible, therefore, to gain this deeper sight or insight if one is not born with it? By no means. This, in fact, is the heart of Mark's good news: that Jesus brings sight to the blind and hearing and speech to the deaf and dumb.

Mark is not a snake-medicine man. A miracle in itself holds diminishing interest for him. What sparks his imagination is the miracle's significance. Mark 2:12 clearly contends that the essential quality of Jesus' miracle-making is its spiritual achievement, not its medicinal value. The miracle of restoring sight to the blind for Mark is far less significant than restoring a lost man to a state of forgiveness. Mark's, and conceivably Jesus', compassion focuses on spiritual more than on physical blindness.

If one reads carefully through Mark 7:31 to 8:26, he may *see* the hidden, the barely visible but dominant motif: hear with your ears and see with your eyes and understand who is in your midst. This " sight and insight " section opens with the story of healing a deaf man and closes with one of healing a blind man. The editorial comment capping the episode is worthy of special attention (ch. 8:37):

They were astonished beyond measure [the most extravagant superlative expression in the entire Gospel], saying, " He has done all things well; he even makes the deaf hear and the dumb speak."

Though the English reader cannot tell, why does Mark speak of the deaf and the dumb here in the *plural*, when the crowd obviously has seen only *one deaf* man healed? Mark may just be generalizing on the scope of Jesus' healing success. Or he may be hinting of a greater miracle, that Jesus brings new vision and hearing to *all* of them.

This latter option seems a likely interpretation, especially since the " sight and insight " theme continues. When the Pharisees seek a sign, Jesus " sighed deeply in his spirit " and said that no sign would be given this generation (ch. 8:11-13). Does Mark imply that Jesus gave no signs, no hints of what he was trying to achieve? Absurd! What Mark and Jesus sigh over is the fact that innumerable signs have been staked all over the course, but that in the country of the blind they do no good.

The moral is driven home quite explicitly in the seafaring discussion that follows. When the disciples press Jesus about their empty bread baskets, Jesus forcibly turns their minds back to the essential fact, their need for spiritual bread:

Why do you discuss the fact that you have no bread? Do you not yet perceive or understand? Are your hearts hardened? Having eyes do you not see, and having ears do you not hear? And do you not remember? (Ch. 8:17-18.)

Mark, in his subtle theological intrusion, adds that the disciples had bread of which they were unaware; Mark begins with the ostensibly trivial comment, " and they had only *one loaf* with them " (v. 14). That one loaf is Jesus, the " bread of life." Mark ties up the tale on " sight and insight " with the story of Peter's receiving his sight, as attested by his confession, " You are the Christ."

Signs and Sight. For Mark, Jesus' life forms a mosaic of intriguing signs. Obsessed with the revelation that Jesus' identity is a mystery revealed to the perspicacious through signs alone, Mark doubles the phenomenon in his own plot. He creates signs for the astute reader with such relish and boundless ingenuity, we cannot afford to bypass them.

Mark's passion for finding and inventing " signs " cannot be exhibited more patently than we find in ch. 13:14:

But when you see the desolating sacrilege set up where it ought not to be (*let the reader understand*), then let those who are in Judea flee to the mountains.

The parenthetical exhortation, " Let the reader understand," waves flags and blows whistles at the reader. " Read carefully here for cues to esoteric meanings." Various explorers in the Marcan territory have uncovered four different species of signs planted in the terrain for the " insight-ed."

1. *Old Testament symbols* offer a logical first selection. Not only does Mark quote the Old Testament to draw attention to its mysterious correlation with New Testament events, but he plays the relationship in looser fashion than this. Relying on his audience's familiarity with the Old Testament, he resorts to the subtle practice of dropping cues. One such cue to a hidden relationship between the Old and New Testament is Mark's sketch of John the Baptist: " Now John was clothed with camel's hair, and had a leather

girdle around his waist " (ch. 1:6). For one who knows his Old Testament well, the image of Elijah immediately pops into focus: " He wore a garment of haircloth, with a girdle of leather about his loins " (II Kings 1:8). Why does Mark wish to connect Elijah with John the Baptist? The answer develops from our knowledge of Jewish Messianic hopes in the first century. Malachi 4:5-6 had predicted that a new Elijah would precede the appearance of the Messiah. Simple logic reveals the propaganda advantage early Christians would have had *if* Jesus were provided with an Elijahlike forerunner. John the Baptist was elected. (Cf. Mark 8:27; 9:9-13; and parallels.)

Allusions to the exodus from Egypt play another significant role in Mark's " sign and sight " theme. Mark intends his reader to notice the similarity of the Lord's feeding Moses in the wilderness and Jesus' feeding the crowds of five and four thousand in " the wilderness." (Cf. Mark 6:42; 8:8; and Ps. 78:29.) A more obscure allusion to the exodus is found in the account of *Jesus' walking on the water*. The first allusion occurs in the words, " Take heart, *it is I* " (Mark 6:50). The Greek for " it is I " reads *ego eimi,* and can also be translated " I AM, " which brings to mind the word of Yahweh to Moses: " Say this to the people of Israel, ' *I AM* has sent me to you ' " (Ex. 3:14). The same expression occurs in the description of Jesus' trial before the high priest. When the priest asks Jesus if he is the Son of the Blessed, he answers, *" Ego eimi "* (Mark 14:62).

A second allusion to the exodus is found in the obvious stylistic similarities between this story and the description of the exodus in Ps. 77:16-20:

> When the waters saw thee, O God,
>> when the waters saw thee, they were afraid,
>> yea, the deep trembled.

> The clouds poured out water;
>> the skies gave forth thunder;
>> thy arrows flashed on every side.
> The crash of thy thunder was in the whirlwind;
>> thy lightnings lighted up the world;
>> the earth trembled and shook.
> Thy way was through the sea,
>> thy path through the great waters;
>> yet thy footprints were unseen.
> Thou didst lead they people like a flock
>> by the hand of Moses and Aaron.

Like the psalmist, Mark joins the exodus motif with a new element, the *Creation motif,* the celebration of God's victory over the powers of the sea and the primordial chaos. Mark combines them, confident that his audience will recognize the relation between Jesus and the God of history and creation.

2. *Typological symbols* are an extended variation on Old Testament symbols, referring to the future as well as to the past. We have already observed how the feeding of the Jews in the wilderness is typologically related to the feeding of the four and five thousand. Mark continues the comparison, adding another typological link pointing to the future.

The feeding of Moses' people in the wilderness	=	The feeding of the four and five thousand by Jesus	=	The feeding of the faithful through the *eucharist* in the wilderness of Rome

Mark indicates this new relation with a passage that sounds like the words of institution for the Lord's Supper. " And he *took the seven loaves,* and *having given thanks* he *broke them* and *gave them* to his disciples to set before the people." The form he uses here would be familiar to every Christian reader of his time; it is the early rendition of the liturgy in Paul where the same sequence of action takes place:

The Lord Jesus on the night when he was betrayed *took bread,* and when he had *given thanks,* he *broke it,* and said, " This is my body which is broken for you." (I Cor. 11:23-24.)

The allusion to the " one loaf with them in the boat " (Mark 8:14) and to the imminent death of Jesus farther on in the context (v. 31) may well be Mark's inventive means of completing the liturgical formulation found in Paul. Jesus is the loaf whose body will be broken in their behalf.

3. *Numbers symbolism* has been the special meat of Austin Farrer. In his *St. Matthew and St. Mark,* Farrer proposes that the numbers involved in the two feedings stories provide the clue to their meaning. Note carefully, Farrer warns us, that the first feeding involves 5,000 people and 12 baskets of crumbs; the second, 4,000 people and 7 baskets. He reminds us that Mark's Hellenistic readers were under the influence of Pythagoreanism and consequently extremely conscious of numbers symbolism. For such readers, the numbers 5, 12, 4, and 7 have special significance. The numbers 5 and 12 are patently Jewish; 5 symbolizes the five books of the Pentateuch, and 12 obviously recalls the tribal structure of Israel. However, the numbers 4 and 7 are typically Hellenistic. The 4 symbolizes many things Greek: the four winds, the four virtues, the four passions, et cetera; the 7 is a number the Pythagoreans especially cherished as witnessed by Philo Judaeus and other Hellenistic writers. That Mark intends his numbers to have symbolic value in the manner Farrer suggests comes out in this statement:

" When I broke the five loaves for the five thousand, how many baskets full of broken pieces did you take up? " They said to him, " Twelve." " And the seven for the four thousand, how many baskets full of broken pieces did you take up? " And they said to him, " Seven." And he said to them, " Do you not yet understand? " (Ch. 8:19-20.)

The verse immediately preceding asks, " Having eyes do you not see, and having ears do you not hear? " (V. 18.)

4. *Name symbolism* is impossible to establish on an unimpeachable basis. Since a given Greek or Aramaic name may have two or three possible meanings, we have no absolute justification for choosing one meaning over another just because it happens to fit the context. In spite of this technical limitation, it seems more than coincidental that Mark chooses certain names to accompany certain events.

An example is the name Bethphage occurring in Mark 11:1 in the context of the story of Jesus' cursing the fig tree. There is little doubt that the story itself is an enacted parable in which the fig tree that bears no fruit is compared with the barrenness of the Jerusalem Temple. Both show all the signs of bearing fruit, but on inspection prove fruitless. Is it accidental that Bethphage means " house of unripe figs "?

Or again, is it totally accidental that the man freed by Pilate is named Barabbas, which means " son of the Father," while the true " son of the Father," the genuine " Barabbas," is crucified in his stead?

5. *Word symbolism* also seems likely in Mark. One such word is the Greek *hodos,* " the way," " road," " journey." In the book of The Acts we find the term used to describe the Christian movement. In Acts 9:2, Paul asks the Jerusalem priesthood for letters to introduce him to the synagogues at Damascus, so that if he finds any " belonging to the Way," men or women, he will bring them bound to Jerusalem. Paul later confesses that he has " persecuted this *Way* to the death " (ch. 22:4) and identifies himself before the governor of Caesarea as a member of " *the Way,* which they call a sect " (ch. 24:14). One of Paul's judges, Felix, is said to have had considerable acquaintance with *the Way* (v. 22), and Paul is described as stirring up no little concern about

the Way (ch. 19:23) when he upsets the silver idol industry in Ephesus.

When Mark speaks of seed falling along the *hodos,* he is likely referring to the weakhearted who are falling along *the Way* (Mark 4:4, 15). John the Baptist is not only preparing for a road and path for the Lord, he is preparing for *the Way* which the Lord's death will precipitate (ch. 1:2-3). When Jesus sends out the Twelve and charges them to take nothing for the *hodos,* he is speaking not only about a " journey," as the RSV translates it, but he is addressing the needs they will face on *the Way* (ch. 6:8). When Mark, who is so clearly preoccupied with the problem of suffering in the life of early Christianity, speaks of the *hodos* which leads to Jerusalem and of the fear that grips the hearts of those who follow (ch. 10:32), he is simultaneously referring to *the Way* which they are all traveling and which may bring each of them to his own Jerusalem. On one occasion the Pharisees make the statement, " Teacher, we know that you are true, and care for no man; for you do not regard the position of men, but truly teach the *hodos* of God." On the basis of the foregoing passages, it appears that Mark's Gospel is an engraved invitation to come along on *the Way* of God, following Christ.

Mark is a master literary strategist. He selects words not only for their denotation, the concrete object they point to, but for their connotation, the inner meaning. Sherman Johnson compares the structure of Mark to " an Oriental rug in which many patterns cross one another." Although Mark's ornate structure does not always provide theological stimulation for a modern reader, for Mark's original readers it supplied an element of style and design without which the fabric as a whole might well have been dull and tasteless. The patterns not only salted the reader's taste, they also stimulated his responsiveness to the question that motivated Mark to write the Gospel: " Who do men say that I am? "

AUTHENTIC EXISTENCE IN MARK

Though Mark might feel awkward with the term " authentic existence," he would not be offended at the idea it conveys. Throughout his Gospel, Mark's controlling interest is *the Way* that leads from the kingdom of men into the " Kingdom of God," from death to life, or in modern terms, from an inauthentic to authentic being.

The story of the young man who asks Jesus, " Good Teacher, what must I do to inherit eternal life? " provides an example of Mark's view of the problem of authentic existence. As the story unfolds (ch. 10:17-31), the questioner turns out to be neither a thief nor a tax collecter, but a " righteous man." After Jesus advises this young man to sell what he has and give to the poor and after the man walks away sorrowfully — he was a man of great possessions — a heated discussion breaks out among the disciples. They challenge Jesus with the question, " Then who can be saved? " The point of the story comes with the following comment, which is frequently ignored, in reading the story, but which Mark regards as the climax: " With men it is impossible, but not with God; for all things are possible with God."

But why, the reader will ask, did Jesus tell the man to liquidate his assets? Why did he let the man walk away sorrowfully, if he seriously believed that " all things are possible with God "? Sorrow was precisely what Jesus was trying to achieve in the young man. Jesus ordered him to do what was constitutionally impossible for him in order to drive him to the despair of self-knowledge.

Mark abhors the " model Christian." The " model Christian " or the perfect religious man doesn't exist, as the story of the young man illustrates. If Mark presents any model of authentic Christianity, it is a parabolically delineated model,

not a statistically charted one. Instead of constructing a catalog of virtues appropriate to the " authentic man," he cites
two general qualities every Christian, *de facto,* shares.

The *quality of faith* distinguishes the authentic from the
inauthentic existent. In his volume entitled *The Problem of
History in Mark*,[9] James Robinson discovers that Mark consistently opposes faith to fear, awe, or astonishment. As the
waves wash over the disciples' boat, Jesus asks: " Why are
you *afraid?* Have you no faith? " (ch. 4:40). When Jesus
heals, the crowds frequently stand about in dumb astonishment or awe, an attitude Mark opposes to faith. Awe, astonishment, or fear is basically the reaction typical of the *spectator* rather than of the *participant.* Like one watching a
sideshow from the bleachers, the faithless man (the specta-
tor-type) watches, observes, even reacts emotionally, but remains safely removed from what he sees. He thinks of what
he sees as " that over there." His reaction is one of objective
astonishment, regarding the object as something which *is* but
which remains foreign, even hostile, to his *existence.* However, the reaction appropriate to faith is one of participation,
involvement, identity, empathy, and " subjective passion."

Faith is also opposed to " sin " in Mark. " Sin " manifests
itself in *two* distinct types. The first is the sin of the obvious
" sinner," the publicly acknowledged violator of religious
law, the prostitute or tax collector, " external sin." The second is the sin of the " internal sinner." Mark also describes
this kind of sin as the *eternal* sin: blasphemy against the
Holy Spirit, namely, the classic Pharisaic sin of spiritual
pride or provincialism (cf. ch. 3:30). " Internal sin," for
Mark, is the lack of readiness to respond to the voice of the
Spirit (the philosopher would say, " voice of truth ") wherever, however, and through whomever it speaks. Mark illustrates this kind of sin by comparing those who hear Jesus
and exclaim, " A new teaching with authority! " (ch. 1:27)

and those who hear Jesus and declare, " He is the son of the devil " (ch. 3:22 f.).

The response of faith that Mark is hoping to cultivate is one of subjective involvement. The Greek verb " to have faith in " (*pisteuein*) connotes trust, involvement, interest, growing out of a sympathetic understanding and natural attraction and affinity. " Loyalty in love " provides a close synonym. The centurion's response to a dying man provides the illustration for faith with his open, unsolicited response of passionate inwardness: " Truly this man was a son of God! " (ch. 15:39). Openness to Jesus does not simply entail acceptance of him as man, or even as God-man; it entails acceptance of what he proclaims about man and about God. From Mark's standpoint, the openness Jesus desires is to a fuller understanding of *oneself* as related to God and to a fuller understanding of *God* as related to oneself.

The venerable Greek motto " Know thyself " provides the beginning of Jesus' message in Mark. The kind of self-knowledge Jesus desired consists of two parts: first, *knowledge of oneself as a sinner,* that is, as one separated from God and in need of repentance (Greek, *metanoesis,* " complete change of mind "). The second part of knowledge that Jesus desires in Mark is the *awareness of oneself as forgiven,* as affirmed by God despite one's flagrant unworthiness. In reading Mark, one begins to surmise that the real miracle lies in Jesus' ability to draw men out of themselves to receive forgiveness.

The sick that Jesus comes to heal are not the deaf, dumb, and leprous patients primarily; he seeks out those lonely men smitten with the *sickness unto death* of which Kierkegaard speaks, men with sickness of the soul. Jesus comes to them because he has hope for them. The contradictory medical practice he employs presupposes that the sickest man may well be closest to health, the principle being that the more one realizes the spiritual vacuum within himself the more apt he is to long to be filled. By the same token the man in gravest peril, spiritually speaking, is the one who is so convinced of his spiritual health that he never takes occasion to discover his partial emptiness. According to Mark, this man, the " righteous," is beyond help because he fails to understand his own need (ch. 2:17). As such he is diametrically opposed to the man of faith.

The *quality of discipleship* is also a characteristic of an authentically existent man. As faith is introspective awareness of one's own being before God, the attitude of *discipleship* is extroverted awareness of one's involvement with other beings before God. The call to discipleship rings down one chapter and up the next in Mark: " Follow me " (chs. 1:17; 2:14; cf. chs. 3:7; 5:24; 6:1; 10:52; 14:54; 15:41).

Jesus never says exactly where he is going. He offers no preflight itinerary. Practically no provision is made for his retinue. They are to take nothing except a staff (ch. 6:8), and few promises are made. The only certain assurance appears to be the inevitability of being delivered to councils and being beaten in synagogues (ch. 13:9). If in the future they find themselves speechless before their accusers, they are ordered to trust in the strange, otherworldly promise that the Holy Spirit will put proper words on their tongues (v. 11). Following Christ precludes the assurance of dignity or even of salvation. The authentic follower must desire only one thing, to lose his life in and with Christ (ch. 8:35). The motto emblazoned on the broadside of this ship of faithful disciples is: " With man it is impossible, but not with God." To the Pelagians, legalists, and religious free enterprisers, this shibboleth is both demoralizing and heretical, for it implies that man can do little to save himself aside from losing himself with no assurance of salvation. When the woman of questionable character parades into Simon's house to break an alabaster jar of extravagant ointment over Jesus' head, she is not commended for the perfection of her act as a consummate expression of a high code of honor. Her commendation is this simple observation: "She has done what she could" (ch. 14:8). Likewise the widow with her mite is commended because "she . . . has put in everything she had, her whole living" (ch. 12:44). The exact sum is infinitely unimportant.

The follower of Jesus lives by no handbook. No master measuring rod is laid across his life. He is measured by the mere fact of his having faith, not by the gross output of his existence. He is judged by his desire to follow, not by the quantity or quality of his religious expression. In existentialist terms, the man of faith in Mark is one who has discovered a truth for himself which he holds in objective uncertainty, but lives with an "infinite passion of inwardness." His one obligation is to respond to the urgency of proclaiming this truth (ch. 1:15).

Mark invites his readers to adventure, not security; to participation, not spectatorship. The Christ he speaks of is not a pastel-tinted figure with gold-leaf trimming; he is more like a Rembrandt or Rouault, not invulnerable, not intimidating, not overwhelming, yet mysteriously and imperiously demanding.

Mark's Gospel is the record of a man who has summoned the totality of basically meager literary skill, "all that he had," to bring his readers to involvement with this man — with the marginal note that a decision about this man marks the line between authentic and inauthentic existence, between life and no-life.

III THE GOSPEL OF MATTHEW:

An Ethical-Apocalyptic Approach

MATTHEW'S JESUS, contrary to Mark's, is hailed, almost as soon as he appears, as the *expected one*. He needs no introduction; the people he comes to save have been awaiting him a long time. Armed with vital bits of evidence from the prophetic writings, they are prepared to identify him immediately as the Messiah (cf. Matt. 2:3-6). As Vincent Taylor remarks, the humanity of Christ so tangible in Mark is beginning to be seen through a doctrinal " veil " in Matthew. This veil bears the indisputable hues of what is commonly referred to in studies of the New Testament era as apocalypticism.

Because apocalypticism contains mixed elements of Persian, Greek, and Hebraic religion, deals with seven-headed beasts and gory visions, and depicts God as the judge who will banish the evil to a hell of eternal fire and send the righteous to eternal bliss, the twentieth-century man has difficulty entering into conversation with this world view.

Though as moderns we have not given up interest in the ideas heaven and hell represent, we are somewhat skeptical about the detailed, technicolor rendition that appears in such books as The Revelation in the New Testament or parts of Daniel in the Old Testament, both excellent examples of apocalyptic thinking. Today we feel a bit uneasy with such literal images. Yet, to understand Matthew's Gospel we must

49

develop a disciplined ear for his language even when it becomes overloaded with apocalyptic images; and we must feel our way into the first-century apocalyptic bent that characterizes the background and substance of his world view.

Benjamin Bacon, in his classical *Studies in Matthew*,[10] concurs that Matthew is " the most apocalyptic of our Gospels "; and he moves from this observation to one even more significant: " If we had no other witness than Matthew's by which to judge of the teaching of Jesus, how different would be our conception! " Bacon is implying that Matthew has inadvertently " twisted the scriptures," to borrow a phrase from S. Vernon McCasland. He has portrayed Christ in apocalyptic garb, because this is the way he sees Christ and this is the kind of imagery his readers understand. The question *we* must raise is whether some slight adjustment must be made in the way we read Matthew if we discover that our way of looking at the world differs from his.

The following pages will attempt to clarify the nature of apocalypticism and how Matthew's specific brand of it has affected his Christian belief. The reader is asked to keep in mind that we will concentrate less on what Matthew has in common with other Gospels than on the special M materials Matthew has added to his Gospel, and the special editorial changes he has made in his sources. We will not attempt to record everything Matthew has recorded, but rather those elements which bear the mark of his creative contribution.

The concluding section will focus on the specific type of Christianity that such a world view appears to engender.

APOCALYPTICISM AND CHRISTOLOGY

To comprehend apocalypticism one must study its historical setting, since apocalypticism seems invariably to break out in times of great personal and communal distress. One of the earliest apocalyptic works, The Book of Daniel, was written about 165 B.C., shortly after the Syrian king, Antiochus Epiphanes IV, who then ruled Palestine, had desecrated the Temple of Jerusalem by sacrificing swine in the sanctuary and erecting a statue of Zeus. Hoping to obliterate Judaic religion, he entered on a campaign to wipe out the practice of circumcision, the reading of the Torah, and the observation of the Sabbath. Thousands of the Jewish males were slaughtered when they refused to heed Antiochus' decree that all people in his kingdom become one in religion, law, and custom.

The Book of Daniel, written by an unknown author, was designed to give courage to his people in this threatening situation. Employing the veiled style of apocalyptic exhortation, he promised his readers through the code of apocalyptic imagery that God would destroy their enemies and grant them eternal life if they would meet this present evil age with faithfulness. Thus, when they read in chapter two of the mighty image that was suddenly shattered by a great stone, they understood that its head of gold signified ancient Babylon; the breasts and arms of silver were Media; its belly and thighs of bronze, Persia; the legs of iron, the kingdom of Alexander the Great; and the feet of mixed iron and clay, the Hellenistic kingdoms of Ptolemy and Antiochus Epiphanes IV. The stone that shattered or would shatter each of these was the Kingdom and might of God.

A special view of history characterizes all apocalyptic thinking. This view might be called the doctrine of the " two ages," according to which history divides into two eras: an evil era, in which the powers of Satan will temporarily be sovereign, and a blissful era, in which God or his representative will speed on the clouds of heaven to slay the forces of evil in heaven and on earth, and to introduce an age of eternal joy for the faithful but eternal perdition for the " sons of darkness." The apocalyptic author rallies his readers for a renewal of courage and " religious determination " in spite of the " gates of hell " which seem to be opening up. Rather than be less " religious," he urges the community to be more so, to bind themselves into one will devoted to practicing the law in every scrupulous detail; having done this, he assures them, they will have qualified themselves as worthy of the grace God will bestow on the Judgment Day.

Practically all the elements found in Daniel, The Revelation, Enoch, II Esdras, and other documents from the ages of apocalyptic writing between 200 B.C. and A.D. 200, are found also in full measure in the Gospel of Matthew. His emphasis on the future and the doctrine of the two ages, his interest in a book of revelations, the emphasis on bracing up the ethical life, and the binding together of the community provide the background against which the life of Jesus is projected in Matthew. Let us now look at each of these dimensions — the futuristic, the Scriptural, the ethical, and communal — noting how they affect Matthew's conceptualization of Jesus.

The Futuristic Dimension: Jesus and the Son of Man. Whereas in Mark the center of history is the moment of Jesus' crucifixion; in Luke, the dispensation of the Spirit in Jesus and on Pentecost; in John, the incarnation of the Word — in Matthew, the center of history lies in the future, the Day of Judgment.

Matthew's preoccupation with everlasting life and eternal perdition steps out from the Gospel in every direction. We find it in his parables and in his apocalyptic editorializations. Some of the special *parables* that reveal Matthew's futurism are the Last Judgment (Matt. 25:31-46), the tale of the wise and foolish maidens (vs. 1-13), and the parable of the wheat and tares (ch. 13:24-30). To the latter, Matthew attaches an apocalyptic sermon (vs. 37-43), which spells out in careful detail the meaning his readers should find in the parable, namely, that the wheat to be spared is really the righteous community, that the tares represent the community of sinners, and that the lord of the harvest is the Son of Man, a figure familiar to all of them.

Matthew's *editorializations* show an equally apocalyptic bent. Replete with images of the " hell of fire " (ch. 5:22), the " eternal fire " (ch. 25:41), the " furnace of fire " (ch. 13:42), and his unique reference to being cast into outer darkness (chs. 8:12; 22:13; 25:30) where there is weeping and gnashing of teeth (chs. 8:12; 13:42, 50; 22:13; 24:51; 25:30), Matthew more than any other Gospel brings his readers within feeling distance of the blaze that is reserved for the tares and from which the wheat will be spared.

Given Matthew's involvement with the threat and promise of the future, how does he fit Jesus of Nazareth into the scheme? As one might suspect, Matthew projects Jesus into the world of the future by identifying him with that glorious and dreadful apocalyptic figure we first encounter in the apocalypse of Daniel, the Son of Man.

> I saw in the night visions,
>> and behold, with the clouds of heaven
>>> there came one like a son of man,
>> and he came to the Ancient of Days
>>> and was presented before him.
> And to him was given dominion
>> and glory and kingdom,
> that all peoples, nations, and languages
>> should serve him;
> his dominion is an everlasting dominion,
>> which shall not pass away,
> and his kingdom one
>> that shall not be destroyed.
>>>>> (Dan. 7:13-14.)

Taking his cue from this and other depictions found in I Enoch and II Esdras, Matthew declares that Jesus of Nazareth is identical with the Son of Man. Note, for example, the following comparison:

Matt. 16:13b	Mark 8:27b	Luke 9:18b
Who do men say that the *Son of man* is?	Who do men say that I am?	Who do the people say that I am?

Matthew leaves no doubt that Jesus of Nazareth is at the same time the one who will come in glory with his angels (Matt. 25:31) to uproot and burn evildoers, to pay every man his due (chs. 13:41; 16:27), and to sit on his throne of judgment over the twelve tribes of Israel (ch. 19:28; cf. ch. 24:38-39). Above all, Matthew stresses how soon he will be coming: " Truly, I say to you, there are some standing here who will not taste death before they see the Son of man coming in his kingdom " (ch. 16:28); " You will not have gone through all the towns of Israel, before the Son of man comes " (ch. 10:23).

Painting Jesus in these bright colors, Matthew hopes to jolt his audience into consciousness of Jesus' manifest importance. On the one hand, Jesus initiates man into the knowledge of God's requirement for admission into heavenly bliss; beyond this, he is also the one who will examine the heavenly candidates at the Last Day. In identifying Jesus as the Son of Man, a jarring and somewhat ominous symbol for one who holds an apocalyptic world view, Matthew gives expression to his intense conviction that Jesus' teaching is of supreme importance for every man. In Matthew's estimation, if one hopes to enter eternal life, he must live out his present life with at least one foot in heaven; he must attend to the words of Jesus of Nazareth now, if he hopes to prepare for meeting him again when he appears as the Son of Man in awesome grandeur.

The Scriptural Dimension: Jesus and the Messiah. As far as we know, the only apocalypse or " book of mysteries " available to Matthew is the Old Testament. How can the Old Testament be regarded as a thesaurus of ancient secrets when it is clearly a collection of straightforward historical, theological, legal, and poetic materials? The answer is found again in the fact that Matthew is an apocalyptic thinker. As such, he possesses the interpretive know-how to read deep mysteries and hints of the future out of this book.

Before describing this interpretive method, we should note that Matthew reads the Old Testament with such mysterious zeal because he is a devout and learned Jew who regards his particular brand of Judaism to be the only true form; and because he believes he can document this contention from the Torah. Like many other enclaves of Jewish apocalyptics, Matthew and his community consider themselves the defenders of a true Judaism whose rights are being currently usurped by the Jerusalemite priests; and like the others, Matthew believes the proof lies " hidden " in Old Testament prophecy.

That Matthew considers himself thoroughly Jewish is evident throughout the Gospel. Some of the ways in which he reveals this are as follows: he revises the un-Jewish Marcan form of the Decalogue, " *Do not* kill, *Do not* commit adultery," et cetera (Mark 10:19), back to its Judaic form, " *You shall not* kill," et cetera (Matt. 19:18 f.). Second, he feels no necessity, as Mark and Luke have done, to explain the meaning of the Jewish Feast of Unleavened Bread (ch. 26:17; Mark 14:12; Luke 22:7). Third, he chooses to describe the worship of the crowds as glorifying the " God of Israel " (Matt. 15:31). Fourth, in behalf of his Jewish audience, he redeems the anti-Jewish account of the Syrophoenician woman (Mark 7:24-30) with three expert, Judaizing revisions: first, by describing her as a Canaanitess rather than a Greek (Matt. 15:22); second, by putting the Jewish Messianic phrase, " O Lord, Son of David," on her lips (v. 22); and third, by prefacing Jesus' concession to the woman with the strongly pro-Jewish sentiment, " I was sent only to the lost sheep of the house of Israel " (v. 24; cf. ch. 10:5-6).

Likewise, his *hostility to the Jerusalemite hierarchy* is evident, as illustrated in these passages:

> Then the chief priests and the elders of the people gathered in the palace of the high priest, who was called Caiaphas, and took counsel together in order to arrest Jesus. (Ch. 26:3-4.)

On another occasion he impugns the integrity of the chief priests by suggesting that they bribed the guards at Jesus' tomb to spread the rumor that " his disciples came by night and stole him away while we were asleep " (ch. 28:13, 15).

One further point about Matthew's Judaism should be made before we analyze his method of interpreting the Old Testament mysteries, namely, that Matthew is in all probability a *Jewish scribe*. This conjecture is based, first, on the fact that Matthew has written a Gospel; second, on a literary quirk he manifests from time to time. In making a careful Synoptic comparison of Matthew's condemnations of the Jerusalemite circle, we discover this interesting habit. Matthew frequently deletes the word " scribe " from his source, as in the following:

Matt. 26:47	Mark 14:43
. . . Judas came, one of the twelve, and with him a great crowd with swords and clubs, from the chief priests and the elders of the people.	. . . Judas came, one of the twelve, and with him a crowd with swords and clubs, from the chief priests *and the scribes* and the elders.

We find that in at least seven instances Matthew performs this same kind of surgery, extracting the " scribe " from the questionable company of priests, elders, and Pharisees (cf. Matt. 9:11; 21:23; 22:34; 22:41; 23:5-6; 26:3; 27:1; and the parallel passages in Mark). A further example of his pro-scribalism appears in ch. 8:19, where a scribe, of all persons, promises to follow Jesus wherever he goes; also in the closing verse of the Sermon on the Mount, Matthew's editorial comment refers to " their scribes," implying that " other scribes," of a better cast, can be found.

Matthew's basic optimism about scribes in general is clearly reflected in this passage:

Therefore I send you prophets and wise men and scribes, some of whom you will kill and crucify, and some you will scourge in your synagogues and persecute from town to town. (Ch. 23:34.)

Can we doubt that Matthew identifies himself with this new race of scribes, and, as has often been suggested, may even think of himself in terms of the picture in ch. 13:52?

Every scribe who has been trained for the kingdom of heaven is like a householder who brings out of his treasure what is new and what is old.

Matthew brings out of his treasure, the Old Testament, both the old law and prophecies of the new law to come in Jesus the Messiah. But how does Matthew the scribe extract apocalyptic secrets from his Old Testament treasure?

Matthew's method of distilling " mysteries " and " veiled secrets " from the Old Testament is described by Krister Stendahl in *The School of St. Matthew* [11] as the " *pesher* method." Stendahl first discovers this method being employed by the apocalyptic sectarians who wrote the Dead Sea scrolls (or scrolls of Qumrân), and finds every reason to believe that Matthew has adopted the technique for himself. Stendahl, incidentally, suggests the author of Matthew to be a whole " school " of scribes rather than a single individual.

The " *pesher* method " of interpreting Scripture may best

be illustrated from a passage from one of the commentaries found in the Qumrân texts. The word *pesher* is the Hebrew verb used to introduce the commentary; it means, " this refers to such and such," whence follows the commentary or interpretation. The purpose of a commentary, ancient or modern, is to supply an extended interpretation of a given passage. The remarkable feature of the *pesher* commentary is the character of the interpretation it offers, which invariably deals with ideas that are more important for the commentator than for the author who wrote the text. Let us see what the Qumrân interpreter does with Micah 1:6, which reads:

I will turn Samaria into a heap in a field, a place for the planting of a vineyard; and I will roll down her stones into the valley, and uncover her foundations.

The commentary, however, reads as follows (as reconstructed by Gaster):

This refers to the Jerusalemitan priests who are leading God's people astray.   '

This unique method of interpretation transforms Micah into an oracle on modern current events.

Needless to say, this method will raise eyebrows among modern historians. As William Brownlee [12] has observed, the obvious defect is that it often leads to a " forced or abnormal construction of the text." Brownlee finds that the Qumrân scribes have inflicted many abuses on the scriptural text they claim to be interpreting; they have rearranged letters in a word; have substituted letters, or have divided a word unnaturally; have interpreted a word as a symbol of a much broader meaning; or have yoked a passage with another passage from a totally different context to " illumine " its " true " meaning.

Does Matthew practice this kind of interpretation? Stendahl answers, " Yes! " Evidence is found especially in the eleven so-called " formula quotations " in Matthew. The formula quotations are those which introduce an Old Testament prophetic quotation with this statement, or its equivalent: " Then was fulfilled what was spoken by the prophet . . ." (cf. chs. 1:23; 2:6, 15, 18, 23; 4:15-16; 8:17; 12:18-21; 13:35; 21:5; 27:9-10). In each instance, Matthew changes the Old Testament quotation to a greater or lesser degree in order to tailor it as much as possible to fit the life of Jesus.

Compare the following accounts of Jesus' directives to his disciples in preparation for his entry into Jerusalem:

Matt. 21:2	Mark 11:2
Go into the village opposite you, and immediately you will find *an ass tied, and a colt with her;* untie *them* and bring *them* to me.	Go into the village opposite you, and immediately as you enter it you will find *a colt* tied, on which no one has ever sat; untie *it* and bring *it*.

Why does Matthew have the disciples fetch two beasts rather than one? We discover why, when we note Matthew's " formula quotation " a few verses later (v. 5; cf. Isa. 62:11; Zech. 9:9)

> Tell the daughter of Zion,
> Behold, your king is coming to you,
> humble, and mounted on an ass,
> and on a colt, the foal of an ass.

Because Matthew believes this Old Testament text implies two beasts rather than one, he adjusts his version of Mark accordingly. One should also note that Matthew draws his " formula quotation " from two totally unrelated verses with unrelated meanings, paring each of them down a bit to apply neatly to his narrative. Thus, Matthew succeeds in making both the prophecy conform to current history and current history to the word of prophecy.

Matthew's motive for adopting the "*pesher* method" of interpreting the Old Testament is to substantiate his belief that Jesus is the one foretold by this book of mysteries. The term that Matthew and many other Jewish-Christians employ to sum up Jesus' "mysterious" relationship to Old Testament prophecy is the title "Messiah," or, in the Greek, "Christ." As Edward Blair and others observe, the title "Christ" is one of Matthew's favorites; and of sixteen or seventeen occurrences in Matthew, all but five are introduced afresh by Matthew rather than borrowed from his sources.

Who is the Christ? He is the anointed one of God, as the Hebrew *māshīah* denotes. In the minds of Matthew's contemporaries this title would evoke all the images associated with the popular Messianic expectation, the image of the Son of David who would reestablish justice in Zion, the image of the great King. In reading Matthew, we are aware, beginning with the first chapter, that he thinks of Jesus in these terms. The genealogical record (ch. 1:1-17), the story of the Wise Men (ch. 2:1-12), Jesus' entry into Jerusalem (ch. 21:1-9), and the title nailed to the cross, which in Matthew reads, "This is Jesus the King of the Jews" (ch. 27:37), all point to early Christianity's, but especially Matthew's, consciousness of the Messianic qualities of Jesus, that the "hopes and fears of all the years are met" in him, to use the words of Phillips Brooks's carol. To prove to his readers that the God of history has again spoken to Israel, this time through a Son, Matthew employs the "*pesher* method," and in so doing, hopes to lead his readers beyond the proof to a full recognition of the new King himself.

The Ethical Dimension: Jesus and the New Moses. A contemporary spokesman for Reformed Judaism once commented that the difference between the Jew and the Christian lies in the fact that the Jew is frustrated over not being fully man and the Christian is frustrated over not being fully God. Matthew tends to fall somewhere between the two. Although Matthew gives indication of settling more in the Christian than in the Jewish camp in terms of this rabbi's definition, as can be seen in Matthew's citation of the command: "You . . . must be perfect, as your heavenly Father is perfect" (ch. 5:48), one senses that Matthew desires to become *neither man,* whom he regards as hopeless to some extent, *nor God,* whom Matthew regards as totally removed from man. Matthew wishes to become "righteous man," which in terms of his "narrow gate" apocalypticism amounts to a creature somewhat lower than God but considerably higher than the average man.

Matthew's penchant for diatribes and threats leads us to believe that he despairs over mankind in general: "Because wickedness is multiplied, most men's love will grow cold" (ch. 24:12). At best, he hopes his Gospel will reach those few who aspire to the heights of righteousness articulated in the life of Jesus. Like Diogenes in ancient Greece, Matthew is in search of righteous men and is prepared, when he finds one, to instruct him in the "way" of righteousness.

Walter Bundy proposes, in *Jesus and the First Three Gospels,*[13] that Matthew is essentially a catechist. Even his apocalyptic discourse (Matt., chs. 24 and 25) includes so many admonitions and instructions that it can be classified as much a "catechetical complex" as an apocalyptic blueprint. Ethics and apocalyptics, inseparable in Matthew, are the microcosm and macrocosm of his thinking. And the bearer of the ethical standard, the original "teacher of righteousness," for Matthew's community, is Jesus of Nazareth.

In *Jesus in the Gospel of Matthew,*[14] Edward Blair observes that "Jesus appears in the Gospel of Matthew as the world's hierophant," the dispenser of divine, saving knowledge. But as a Jew speaking to a Jewish community, Matthew is deeply conscious of another great hierophant, namely, Moses. Both Moses and Jesus are spokesmen for God (Ex. 4:12-17) in Matthew's estimation; his task is to convince his Jewish audience that Jesus shares the honors. To achieve this, he constructs the biographical suggestion that the two careers are practically identical. As Moses was discovered by Pharaoh's daughter (Ex. 2:5 ff.), Jesus' birth is attended by royalty (Matt. 2:11). As Moses came out of Egypt, so does Jesus (v. 13). Pharaoh's attempt to slay the Hebrew male infants (Ex. 1:16) is matched by Herod's bloodbath (Matt. 2:16). As Moses was on the mountain forty days and nights (Ex. 24:18) and as the people of Israel were in the wilderness forty years (Num. 14:33), so Jesus was tempted forty days and nights (Matt. 4:2). The dispensation of the law on Mount Sinai by Moses (Ex., ch. 20) is now fulfilled in the new law which Jesus gives on the mount (Matt., chs. 5 to 7).

Benjamin Bacon was perhaps the first to propose that the trunk of Matthew's literary corpus consists of five books, which to a Jew would suggest the five books of Moses:

Book I   Chs. 3 to 7   On Discipleship
Book II   Chs. 8 to 11:1   On Apostleship
Book III Chs. 11:2 to 13:52   On the Hidden Teaching
Book IV   Chs. 13:53 to 19:1   On Church Administration
Book V   Chs. 19:2 to 26:1   On the Last Things

As Moses spoke with God " mouth to mouth, clearly, and not in dark speech " (Num. 12:8), so Jesus knows and is known by the Father in a unique way (Matt. 11:25 ff.). The " yoke " of the law which Moses laid upon Hebraic shoulders (Sir. 51:26) is replaced with the easy yoke of one who is gentle and lowly in heart (Matt. 11:28-30). As Moses and the Children of Israel are fed the bread of heaven in the wilderness (Ex. 16:4), so Jesus and the five thousand are fed in the wilderness (Matt. 14:13-21; 15:32-39). Both Jesus and Moses make their final appearance on a mountain (ch. 28:16; Deut. 34:1).

Perhaps a passage that most precisely illustrates Matthew's understanding of the Moses-Jesus continuum is the noted M statement on Jesus and the law:

Think not that I have come to abolish the law and the prophets; I have come not to abolish them but to fulfil them. For truly, I say to you, till heaven and earth pass away, not an iota, not a dot, will pass from the law until all is accomplished. Whoever then relaxes one of the least of these commandments and teaches men so, shall be called least in the kingdom of heaven; but he who does them and teaches them shall be called great in the kingdom of heaven. For I tell you, unless your righteousness exceeds that of the scribes and Pharisees, you will never enter the kingdom of God. (Matt. 5:17-20.)

Immediately following are a series of six antitheses that begin with the formula, " You have heard that it was said to the men of old, . . . but I say to you. . . ." The authority of the old Moses is equated with that of the new, if not superseded by it.

Though this passage may well be an authentic statement of Jesus', we must ask what it meant to Matthew and how it relates to other Matthean ideas. The key to Matthew's construction probably lies in the last statement, " Unless your righteousness exceeds that of the scribes and Pharisees, you will never enter the kingdom of God." The one thing needful in Matthew's estimation is *righteousness*. This is seen in Matthew's habit of forcing the word " righteous " or " unrighteousness " into his script whenever convenient. For example, Jesus explains his motive for being baptized by John as the desire " to fulfil all *righteousness* " (ch. 3:15). Second, to the command, " Seek first his kingdom," Matthew adds, " and his *righteousness* " (ch. 6:33). Third, Matthew describes heaven as the place where " the *righteous* will shine

like the sun " (ch. 13:43). Fourth, the Last Day is charac-
terized as the occasion for angels to " separate the evil from
the righteous " (v. 49). Other instances of editorial insertion
of these terms are chs. 10:41; 13:17; 21:32; 23:29, 35. Jesus has come to give birth to a community of the " righteous."

Of what does *righteousness* consist? Obviously it does not
involve the rejection of the old law. Jesus does not reject
Moses' seat; rather, those who sit on it and who fail to practice what they preach (ch. 23:2 ff.). Jesus doesn't destroy
the law; he supports it. He even supports the dietary and
cultic law; the scribes are condemned, not because they
" tithe mint and dill and cummin," but because they " have
neglected the weightier matters of the law . . . ; these you
ought to have done, without neglecting the others " (v. 23;
cf. chs. 24:20; 15:17 vs. Mark 7:19).

If anything, the *righteousness* that Matthew conceives demands outdoing the Pharisees and scribes, exceeding what
they have done. The New Moses in Matthew is a proponent
of " excessive righteousness," which is constituted in part by
a *spiritualizing or deepening of the commandment;* lusting
after a woman or hating is as evil as adultery or killing
(Matt. 5:21 ff.). It consists also of a kind of " selective legalism," choosing one Old Testament principle over another
(cf. v. 38). When Jesus is asked which commandment is the
greatest, his answer in Matthew provides telling comparison
with Mark and Luke. All three report the " love-God, love-
neighbor rule," then add:

Matt. 22:40	Mark 12:31	Luke 10:28
On these two com-mandments depend all the law and the prophets.	There is no other commandment greater than these.	You have answered right; do this, and you will live.

Only in Matthew does Jesus explicitly *select* two principles as the basis of the whole law. Above all, the new righteousness consists of *good deeds,* of " fruit-bearing " (Matt. 7:15-20; 12:33-35), and of *practice* along with preaching (ch. 23:2). The parable of the two sons, recorded only in Matthew (ch. 21:28-32), contrasts a son who first refuses to work in the vineyard but in the end does, with one who at first promises to go but in the end refuses. The first one receives the praise as he who " did the will of his father." That man who *performs* as well as teaches the commandments " shall be called great in the kingdom of heaven " (ch. 5:19; cf. ch. 25:31-46).

According to the New Moses in Matthew, the highest motivation for the righteous life is the promise of reward, or negatively, the threat of judgment. Here again ethics and apocalyptics prove to be inseparable. The word " reward " (Greek, *misthos*) occurs once in Mark, three times in Luke, and *ten* times in Matthew (chs. 5:12, 46; 6:1, 2, 5, 16; 10:41 twice, 42; 20:8), and in no other book of the New Testament more than twice. Unlike Mark's Jesus who offers few concrete assurances to the man who follows him, the New Moses in Matthew spells out the options, prerequisites, and consequences rather unambiguously. Matthew's New Moses brings hope to his apocalyptically anxious life by answering, once and for all, the crucial question, " What good deed must I do, to have eternal life? " (cf. ch. 19:17; Mark 10:17; Luke 18:19). The answer, which Matthew's Gospel is intent on elaborating, is: exceed the righteousness of the scribes and Pharisees.

The Communal Dimension: Jesus and Emmanuel. The greenhouse for " excessive righteousness " is the " church," a term that only Matthew among the Synoptics uses (Matt.

16:18; 18:17). Like the apocalyptics before him, Matthew solves the problem of widespread individual and corporate evil with the proposal that goodness can be achieved only in communal isolation, away from society's mainstream. Isaiah and Jeremiah referred to groups who practiced such moral and religious isolation as the " remnant." The Psalms called them the *tsaddiqim*, " the righteous ones." Later Judaism employed the term *hasidim*, " the loyal ones." Others called them the people of the ghetto. And early Christianity called itself the " church," interpreted by some to mean " those who were called out " (Greek, *ekklēsia*) of society into a *communio sanctorum*, a holy society.

Although, from Matthew's point of view, the main occupation of the community is to await the imminent coming of the Son of Man (ch. 10:23), they are temporarily responsible to conduct themselves in an orderly and righteous fashion, until the end actually comes. For this temporary provision the disciples, especially Peter, James, and John, and presumably their appointed successors are given the authority to " bind and loose " on earth and heaven, to acquit or condemn offenders (chs. 16:18-20; 18:15-20). Matthew and the group of scribes he represents have as their task the production of a manual of discipline, instruction, liturgy, and homiletic discourse for the community. For these and other reasons, F. C. Grant has called Matthew " the ecclesiastical Gospel par excellence."

Although considerable moral and temporal power is invested in the church hierarchy, Matthew hopes to make clear that the officials of the church have not arrogated this authority. The authority ultimately rests in Jesus, as is made plain in his farewell discourse:

All authority in heaven and on earth has been given to me. Go therefore and make disciples of all nations, baptizing them in the name of the Father and of the Son and of the Holy Spirit, teaching them to observe all that I have commanded you; and lo, I am with you always, to the close of the age. (Ch. 28:18-20.)

From Matthew's standpoint, the community's obligations to the risen Christ include: first, the recognition of his cosmic authority; second, the proclamation of this authority; third, the teaching of the New Torah to all men; and fourth, the acknowledgment of Jesus' presence in their midst.

The last note comes as a new and somewhat surprising element in the context of Matthew's apocalypticism. However, in ch. 18:20 we also read, " Where two or three are gathered in my name, there am I in the midst of them." Is Matthew implying, as Helen Milton has suggested in her article " The Structure of the Prologue to St. Matthew's Gospel," that the angelic prophecy of a child named Emmanuel, " God with us " (Greek, *meth' hēmōn*), has now been fulfilled in the promise of the resurrected Jesus to be " with you " always (Greek, *meth' hymōn*)? Is Matthew proposing that the present link between the Jesus of the past and the Son of Man in the future is Jesus Emmanuel? One suspects that this may be the case. In any event, the problem must have been difficult for Matthew and his community. Luke solves it with the ascension story, implying that Jesus' place is at the right hand of the Father until he comes again in glory. Paul comes to a similar solution, though he also speaks of being " in Christ " in the present, or of Christ's being " in me." Matthew, however, seems to favor the solution of the problem through the image of " God with us "; he declares Jesus to be present in the community in a quasi-divine sense.

The peculiar use of the verb *proskyneō*, " to kneel before," or " to worship," may provide a clue to Matthew's understanding of Jesus' place in the community " between the times." In no other New Testament book, with the exception of one verse in John (ch. 9:38), is this verb used in relation to Jesus. Ordinarily the verb denotes "worship," either of God or of false gods. Yet in Matthew we find that the Wise Men (ch. 2:2, 8, 11), the leper (ch. 8:2), a ruler (ch. 9:18), the disciples in the boat (ch. 14:33), the mother of the sons of Zebedee (ch. 20:20), the women at the tomb (ch. 28:9), and the eleven disciples on the mount of departure (v. 17) are all said to have " knelt down " before Jesus, which in the New Testament context almost certainly connotes the idea that they worshiped him.

Does this mean that Matthew proposes complete identity of Jesus with God the Father? By no means. Matthew, like Paul (I Cor. 15:26-28), leaves unmistakable evidence of the line that separates the great God from Jesus his anointed one. The term " father," which appears in Matthew twice as often as in any other Gospel, is used by Jesus himself with the self-evident implication that the Father supersedes the Son. In Matt. 23:9, Jesus tells his disciples, " Call no man your Father on earth, for you have one Father, who is in heaven." In ch. 26:53, Jesus states explicitly that the Father is his protector who will send him twelve legions of angels if necessary. For Matthew, God is " the great King " (ch. 5:35) and Jesus is his Son, his representative, his spokesman, and his appointed judge.

The closest we may come to an accurate description of Matthew's Christology is that Jesus is a middle figure, an intermediary or intercessor. This analysis is borne out by the following two passages, especially. " Every one who acknowledges me before men, *I* also will acknowledge before *my Father who is in heaven;* but whoever denies me before men, *I* also will deny before *my Father who is in heaven."* (Matt. 10:32-33.) The second passage reads, " All things have been delivered to me by my Father; and no one knows the Son except the Father, and no one knows the Father except the Son and any one to whom the Son chooses to reveal

him." (Matt. 11:27, Q.) Though Jesus is clearly differen-
tiated from the Father, at the same time he speaks from a
singularly close relation to him. To have such a man in the
midst of one's community is, without exaggerating the religious conviction of Matthew or perhaps of any Christian at
any time, equivalent to having " God with us." This is simply
another way of expressing the doctrine of the incarnation,
the conviction, to employ Paul's terminology, that " God was
in Christ " (II Cor. 5:19).

Although the *function* of " Emmanuel " seems clear in
Matthew, his *nature* lacks specific definition, probably because Matthew believes the coming of the Son of Man will
eliminate the necessity for such definition. What is Emmanuel for Matthew? Is he angel, man, or a totally unique
kind of creature? Though we cannot answer these questions
with certainty, we can point to at least one likely answer.

The apocalyptic literature of Matthew's period, especially
that in Qumrân, provides Matthew with a ready-made image
to describe the person and work of Jesus as the Emmanuel.
This figure is the archangel. The Testament of Dan.,[15] 6:2,
describes Michael thus:

The angel that intercedeth for you; he is a mediator between
God and man, and for the peace of Israel he shall stand up against
the Kingdom of the enemy.

In the Dead Sea scrolls, Michael or perhaps Uriel is identified as the " prince of light " or the " spirit of truth " whose
function is to abide in the community, protecting its members from the " spirit of perversity " and instructing them
in righteousness. In the Qumrân scroll entitled " War of the
Sons of Light and the Sons of Darkness," we find this description of Michael:[16]

He [God] will send eternal help to the lot he has redeemed by
the power of the angel he has made glorious for rule, Michael, in
eternal light, to give light in joy to all Israel, peace and blessing

to the lot of God, to exalt among the gods the rule of Michael and the dominion of Israel over all flesh. (xvii. 6-8, Burrows' translation.)

In *More Light on the Dead Sea Scrolls*,[17] Millar Burrows lists the epithets commonly applied to the angels: "Holy Ones," "Glorious Ones," "Sons of Heaven," "Host of Heaven," "Mighty Ones." Included in the list is the surprising title "Gods" (Hebrew, *elim*). Each of the four archangels, Michael, Gabriel, Raphael, Sariel or Uriel (the name of the fourth archangel appears to have been flexible), has a name that ends in the suffix "el," the Hebrew word for God (Michael = "Who is like God?"; Uriel = "God is my light"; et cetera).

It may be that in employing the name "Emmanuel," Matthew is toying with the archangelic image as a useful symbolic vehicle to express Jesus' relation to the community during the interim. In any event, we can observe that Matthew's conception of the interim Jesus as "God with us" approximates the Qumrân conception of the angels or "messengers" of God. As Sons of Heaven, Glorious Ones, and Gods, they make their divine presence felt in the midst of the community who have cut themselves off from the world in the hope of being found clothed in robes of righteousness (cf. Matt. 22:11-14) when the Son of Man comes to judge. Having "God with them," Matthew's community prepares to preach the "gospel of the Kingdom . . . throughout the whole world, as a testimony to all nations; and then the end will come" (ch. 24:14).

THE APOCALYPTIC TEMPERAMENT IN MATTHEW

The Gospel of Matthew, like most apocalyptic literature, is born out of insecurity. Though Matthew shares with us some of the most moving literature in the New Testament, we cannot avoid the impression that he writes for the specific purpose of supplying theological and psychological security to an island of anxious Jewish-Christian apocalyptics rather than for the purpose of creating an eternally classic document for a continuing Christianity. Matthew is writing in the conscious shadow of the end. In the fear of current historical threats and of eternal perdition, and with a thirst for righteousness and a longing for eternal joy, he is urging his community to dig in, to nail down the shutters, to secure themselves with greater deliberation than ever against the present storm, and to trust that God will bring them to their reward.

Strange as it may seem, Matthew is not a God-*centered* Gospel. Though Matthew assumes that God is to be praised as creator, sustainer, and King of the universe, he does not dedicate his Gospel to the elaboration of this fact, as, for instance, The Psalms do. Matthew *centers* his concern on other, more immediate and pressing matters. Nor does Matthew appear to be a Christ-*centered* Gospel. Though Matthew regards the Christ (and Son of Man, New Moses, and Emmanuel) as one who brings invaluable new knowledge of sin and righteousness, provides directives for perfection (ch. 5:48) and assurances for the future, still it is Jesus' *message,* not Jesus himself, that speaks to Matthew's ultimate concern.

The subject of Matthew's ultimate concern is salvation, not as a theological concept, but as a personal reality, of immediate personal importance.

As an apocalyptically tempered individual, Matthew is interested in exploring the nature of God and Jesus only insofar as they relate to the problem of the *saved man,* to the loss he may suffer from unrighteousness, and to the eternal gain he may achieve through long-suffering righteousness. What keeps Matthew awake nights, we might suspect, is not a theological but a supremely practical problem: how and when his beloved community will be rescued from this evil age.

The dot at the center of Matthew's world is the righteous man. Naturally this pervasive man-centeredness will leave its mark on his concept of the social and intellectual character of the church. It is visible especially in Matthew's tendency toward *exclusivism, pragmatic conservatism,* and *Christological orthodoxy.*

Matthew's *exclusivism* blows up the image of the " outsider," the Gentile (ch. 6:7, 32), the tax collector (ch. 18:17), the Pharisee, and the sinner as a subversive threat. To avert contamination, the Christian is to become an " insider," marked by perfection (ch. 19:17, 21) and fruitfulness (ch. 21:41). In a deceptive and treacherous world, the Matthean recluses are to be as " wise as serpents and innocent as doves " (ch. 10:16). Whereas Mark advises his readers to throw caution to the winds and forget themselves, Matthew recommends that they build themselves houses of mirrors to ensure morally impeccable living (cf. ch. 22:11-14).

Matthew's *pragmatic conservatism* is apparent in his partiality for the conservative virtues as the standard Christian diet. These include meekness (ch. 5:5), purity (v. 8), pacifism (vs. 9, 11), and humility (ch. 18:3). The peacemaker (ch. 5:9) is the ideal man. Matthew abhors conflict, at least on a this-worldly, physical level. This distaste for the unpleasant may explain Matthew's version of the following statement, which eliminates the abrasive quality of Luke's:

Luke 14:26	Matt. 10:37
If any one comes to me and does not *hate* his own father and mother and wife . . . , he cannot be my disciple.	He who loves father or mother more than me is not worthy of me.

The word "pragmatic" applies to Matthew's conservatism because he values these virtues for the work they can accomplish, rather than for what they are in themselves. For example, "childlikeness" is encouraged as a means to another end, as is seen in this comparison:

Matt. 18:3-4	Mark 10:15 = Luke 18:17
Unless you turn and become like children, you will never enter the kingdom of heaven. Whoever humbles himself like this child, he is the greatest in the kingdom of heaven.	Whoever does not *receive* the kingdom of God like a child shall not enter it.

Matthew has turned the Marcan emphasis on *receiving* the Kingdom to an emphasis on developing the prerequisite virtue for entrance. He is recommending the conscious cultivation of humility as a self-saving device. Likewise in the Beatitudes one is urged to cultivate the "virtue" cited in the first half of each Beatitude in order to achieve the "reward" cited in the second, viz., "Be merciful" to obtain mercy (v. 7). As we noted in the first chapter, the highly polished liturgical form of the Beatitudes, not to mention the fact that practically all of them are M passages, suggests that they represent more the *pragmatic conservatism* of Matthew than the idealistic radicalism of Jesus.

Christological orthodoxy is a natural companion to apocalypticism and its man-centeredness. Neither the person of Jesus nor his teachings are safe in a world that tolerates the coexistence of truth and falsehood, of righteousness and evil. To protect them, it is necessary, as the Rabbinic Jews discovered, to "build fences." Even a quick reconnaissance of Matthew reveals signs of Christological fence-building. One notices this in a subtle way with Matthew's tendency to *objectify* Jesus, for example, in Matthew's rendition of the baptism. Notice Matthew's " speech from heaven " in comparison with Mark and Luke:

Matt. 3:17	Mark 1:11 = Luke 3:22
This is my beloved Son, with *whom* I am well pleased.	*Thou* art my beloved Son; with *thee* I am well pleased.

In Mark and Luke, God addresses Jesus personally. In Matthew, he makes an indirect and impersonal proclamation *about him* to the crowd.

Another kind of fence-building is the system of proofs that Matthew erects to defend Jesus against suspicion and cynicism. The legendary elements of the birth stories are introduced as proof of his divine origin, his descendance from David, and as noted earlier, his typological relationship to Moses (cf. chs. 1 and 2). The legendary accounts of Pilate's wife's dream of Jesus' innocence (ch. 27:19), the opening of the tombs at Jesus' crucifixion (vs. 51-53), and the bribing of the soldiers (vs. 62-66; ch. 28:11-15) serve similar defensive purposes. Matthew is the first of the Gospel writers to develop the sinlessness of Jesus as a Christological proof (ch. 3:14-15). On one occasion he depicts Jesus as a bit of a wizard who directs the disciples to catch a fish and pay the Temple tax with the shekel in its mouth (ch. 17:24-27).

As an orthodox institution, Matthew's church is dedicated not to involvement in the world but to dissemination of its truths, definition of its teachings, defense of its Christological dogma, and preservation of its " mysteries " (cf. ch. 13:11 vs. Mark 4:11). It may be that in their hostile environment they had no option but to build theological ramparts, and it may be, that had Matthew's community and others not defined their Christology, even at the cost of becoming inflexible, the " good news " might have been dissipated in the milling crowds of theologies and theosophies that overpopulated the Mediterranean countries in the first century.

In any event, we have Matthew's offering, the product of a mind passionate in teaching and apocalyptically anxious in living. As an apocalyptic he has succeeded, for better or worse, in planting his world view in the minds of twenty centuries of Christians, though in the past century this world view has been seriously challenged.

As teacher and ethicist, however, Matthew has been most successful. For many centuries Matthew's treasury of liturgical and didactic masterpieces have qualified him as the apple of the church's eye. How easy it is to sit at the feet of such a skillful master, neat, orderly, rich in illustration, averse to ambiguity, ethically straightforward, and sufficiently threatening to ensure alert learning. Yet to appreciate fully what he, or any great teacher for that matter, has to say, it behooves us to listen to him with a maturity that is as sensitive and attentive to the limitations of his perspective as to the heights of his insight. When this occurs, Matthew will be transformed from the role of " authoritarian figure " in the church to the much-needed role of " fellow Christian " with whom Christians of any age can enter into dialogue, over the nature of the man whom Matthew, speaking as an ethical-apocalyptic figure, chooses to call Son of Man, Messiah, Teacher, and Emmanuel.

IV THE GOSPEL OF LUKE:

An Aesthetic-Historical Approach

PHILOSOPHIES of history come packaged in various sizes and shapes, and everyone has one. From the simple remark, "Everything will turn out all right," to the complicated dialectical materialism of Marx, a theory of history is in operation. There are historical pessimisms and optimisms, determinisms and voluntarisms, passivisms and activisms, and somewhere in one of these " isms " every man can be found.

The Bible, perhaps more than any comparable collection, bespeaks a surprising variety of historical world views: the skepticism of Ecclesiastes, the pragmatism of Deuteronomy, and the theological optimism of Second Isaiah. The New Testament shares this variety, with Paul's quasi-predestinarianism, Matthew's apocalypticism, and John's dualism. But perhaps the literary award for the most highly developed philosophy of history in the New Testament should go to the author of Luke-Acts, the two-volume work that constitutes about one fourth of the total New Testament literature.

Luke is the philosopher of history par excellence among the Gospel writers. Matthew, to be sure, presupposes a clearcut concept of history, but never bothers to spell it out, assuming that his apocalyptic audience already shares it. Mark, in an existential-like stance, shows little historical interest in breadth, preferring to concentrate on the narrower history of the individual as he " follows Christ." And the Gospel of John follows, more or less, the Marcan pattern. But when we approach Luke we discover a thoroughly and explicitly historical mind, intent on mapping out the whole of his experience in a master plan. With the intellectual vigor of a Hegel, Luke insists that faith and historiography are inseparable. The meaning of Christ, of God, and of the Spirit cannot be perceived apart from the historical understanding of Christ as the center link in a comprehensive divine plan, of God as the creator and executor of the plan, and of the Spirit as the sustainer of the plan in each of its epochs.

Opposed to Mark, who sounds a call for decision, and to Matthew, who demands stern perseverance and rigid obedience, Luke presses his audience for an intellectual, aesthetic, and religious appreciation of the intricate splendor and " saving " magnificence of God's plan. Luke is not only a marveling intellectual; he is also a broadly humanitarian thinker and a lofty idealist with a vision of universal religion. Yet it is qua historian that Luke is able to draw these interests together. Though molded by the Greek historiography in his youth, Luke has been tutored in his maturity by the Hebrew mind, by Isaiah, by the psalmist, and by the massive Old Testament theologies of history. Luke's world, the one to which he would introduce his reader, stands on three Judeo-Hellenistic pillars: on God its Lord, on God's " anointed one " its emissary of " salvation," and on God's Spirit its perennial source of power.

GOD AND HISTORY: THE PAST AND THE PRESENT

Whether any historians are 100 percent antiquarian is questionable; certainly Luke is not. His interest in history emerges from his involvement with the present. And the problem in the present that preoccupies him is the gradual infiltration of Christianity into the Gentile world and the anxiety and resistance this move has created among those who want Christianity to remain an unspoiled child of Judaism.

Since the destruction of Jerusalem some fifteen or twenty years earlier, Luke, and many other Hellenistic Jews, grew in the conviction that Christianity was more than a Jewish sect. Following in the intellectual footsteps of the apostle Paul, Luke deems Christianity to have the potential and the promise of becoming a universal religion. But many do not. They prefer to believe that in order to preserve the integrity of Christianity, new Christians are not to receive the baptism of Christ until after they have accepted the signs of Moses, circumcision and the law.

Over against these Judaizers, Luke defends the growing policy of including the Gentiles without insisting on their Judaization. Arguing from scripture and the " testimony of the Spirit " as his authorities, Luke sketches a theology of history, showing how the prophetic heritage of Israel and of Christ leave no alternative but to affirm the present age as that time which God has set aside for the sake of the Gentiles (Luke 21:24).

Luke is undeniably a rhetorical historian, as F. C. Grant tells us. The mark of the rhetorician, as opposed to the objective or entertaining historian, is that he uses history to advocate a cause or prove a case. History for him is neither the simple enumeration of data nor a series of amusing anecdotes, but the school in which one learns to live more profitably in the present.

The speeches in the book of The Acts are Luke's sounding board for his rhetorical interpretation of history. Though his Gospel provides many hints of his scheme, the book of The Acts is the most valuable and voluble source to the point. These speeches in The Acts number about twenty-four. Eight of them are attributed to the apostle Peter; nine to Paul; one to James the brother of Jesus; one to Stephen; and five to non-Christians: the venerable rabbi Gamaliel, Demetrius the silversmith of Ephesus, the Ephesian town clerk, Tertullus who accuses Paul before Felix, and Felix' successor, Porcius Festus.

Like Tacitus, Josephus, and Thucydides, noted historians in the Greco-Roman era, Luke too uses his speeches to expound his own ideas more than those of the presumed speaker. The reason for this Martin Dibelius points out in his article " The Speeches in Acts and Ancient Historiography ": [18]

> The ancient historian was not aware of any obligation to reproduce only, or even preferably, the text of a speech which was actually made; perhaps he did not know whether a speech was in fact made at the time; sometimes he did know, but he did not know the text of it; perhaps he could not have known it if the speech was made, for example, in the enemy's camp to a limited audience.

The ancient historian's purpose in speech-recording was, first, to measure carefully his knowledge of the general character of the speaker and the dynamics of the situation; second, to work out his own ideas on how the event fits into the broader scope of things as he sees it; and third, to compose a speech giving due consideration to all three elements, especially the third. In Luke's case, that third element is " the plan."

The Plan. Three words or types of words provide the birthmarks of Luke's plan. They are the Greek terms: *boulē, dei,* and a family of words all of which begin with the preposition *pro*. These three have two characteristics in common: they all convey the idea of historical necessity, and they are all found preeminently in Luke-Acts, seldom elsewhere in the New Testament.

The first word, *boulē*, means " plan." It occurs ten times in Luke-Acts (Luke 7:30; 23:51; Acts 2:23; 4:28; 5:38; 13:36; 19:1; 20:27; 27:13, 42), and in each instance is dressed in full theological regalia as a vehicle for Luke's theological historiography. Peter's Pentecost speech provides an example:

> Men of Israel, hear these words: Jesus of Nazareth, a man attested to you by God with mighty works and wonders and signs which God did through him in your midst, as you yourselves know — this Jesus, delivered up according to the definite plan [*boulē*] and foreknowledge [*prognōsis*] of God, you crucified and killed by the hands of lawless men. But God raised him up, having loosed the pangs of death, because it was not possible for him to be held by it. (Acts 2:22-24.)

The theological implications of this speech are almost sensational for Luke's audience. To a community hard put to explain Jesus' violent and ignominious death, Luke proclaims that the death was an expression of God's plan and not the product of mute and ruthless historical causes. This means that the Christian is not to regard Christ's death as a tragedy, as many did, but as an occasion of God's redemption, comparable to the redemptive acts of the Suffering Servant described in Isa. 52:13 to 53:12. For the early Christians who found themselves in intellectual and theological difficulty over this problem, Luke's interpretation comes as the long-awaited hypothesis that explains the tangle of previously unrelated and inexplicable facts.

The second word, *dei*, can be translated " it is necessary " or " one must." Occurring forty-four times in Luke-Acts, this word is used by Luke to elucidate the " divine mustness " of past events. Not only was it " necessary " for Jesus as a child to argue with the scribes in the Temple (Luke 2:49), but also to preach in city after city (ch. 4:43), to suffer and be rejected, killed, and on the third day raised (chs. 9:22; 17:25; 24:7-26; Acts 17:3), because it was "necessary" for scripture to be fulfilled (Luke 22:37; 24:44). In like fashion it was "necessary" for Judas to die the way he did (Acts 1:16), and for Paul to suffer (ch. 9:16) and finally to testify in Rome before Caesar, as he had in Jerusalem (chs. 23:11; 27:24).

The third set of words, the *pro* words, translated as "fore-knowledge" (Acts 2:23), "foreordain" (ch. 4:28), "fore-tell" (ch. 1:16), "proclaim beforehand" (ch. 13:24), add to Luke's symphony on divine necessity. To the thesis that God constantly guides history, Luke adds that he announces beforehand what he will do through his prophets and through Christ, so that when these things are accomplished men might know that it is he who has ordained them.

With this thesaurus of words, Luke declares history to be, not the progeny of chance, but the child of God's making. Luke does not imply that human freedom and the "law" of cause and effect are thereby annulled. What it does imply is that in spite of these principles, or perhaps through them, the prior principle of the redemptive will of God will never fail to find expression.

Times and Seasons. As the curtain rises in The Acts, the disciples are being told something that Luke knows will interest his "eavesdropping" audience:

> It is not for you to know times or seasons which the Father has fixed by his own authority. But you shall receive power when the Holy Spirit has come upon you; and you shall be my witnesses in Jerusalem and in all Judea and Samaria and to the end of the earth. (Acts 1:7-8.)

With these words Luke begins to outline the plan. He begins by advising his readers that although there is little point in trying to figure out the " times and seasons " of the *far-distant* future, there is point in contemplating the "times " predicted by Jesus for the *near* future and the times, the " allotted periods " (Acts 17:26) already unfolded, in the recent and distant past.

Following the general time scheme blueprinted by Hans Conzelmann in his comprehensive *The Theology of St. Luke*,[19] let us examine Luke's three-stage plan: the time of Israel, the time of Christ, and the time of the Gentiles.

The *time of Israel* has this legend inscribed upon it: " The law and the prophets were until John " (Luke 16:16). On a theoretical basis, this period of the Law and the Prophets provides Luke with two insights: that history is the locus of God's mighty acts, and that men are the media of God's prophetic words. On a practical basis, the significance of this period for Luke's theology of history lies in the testimony that Moses, David, Samuel, and John the Baptist make in anticipation of the second stage, the time of Christ.

The *time of Christ*, " the time that the Lord Jesus went in and out among us " (Acts 1:21), is not an occasion of lamentation but of rejoicing for Israel. It might be compared to a wedding feast, an image Luke enjoys. God is not about to lose a daughter (Israel) but to gain a son (the Gentiles). The time of Christ marks the marriage of the Gentiles into the family of God. To be sure, some of the relatives will not approve and may refuse to come to the wedding; but Luke insists that the coming of Christ is for Israel's glory, not for her diminution. As Simeon says, holding the young child Jesus in his arms (Luke 2:29-32):

> Lord, now lettest thou thy servant depart in peace,
> according to thy word;
> for mine eyes have seen thy salvation
> which thou hast prepared in the presence of all peoples,
> a light for revelation to the Gentiles,
> and for glory to thy people Israel.

The time of Christ is the center of history, on the one hand fulfilling the time of Israel, and on the other, introducing the time of the Gentiles.

The *time of the Gentiles* has as its theme, " From Jerusalem to Rome." Luke cues his readers in on this itinerary with the promise of the risen Christ to his disciples, that they shall receive the Spirit and be his " witnesses in *Jerusalem . . . Judea . . . Samaria* and to the end of the earth " (Acts 1:8).

Luke intends to take these geographical items quite seriously, as prophecies that must be fulfilled. With clever, yet sufficiently noticeable editorial insertions in the narrative of The Acts, Luke shows, station by station, how the prophecy is being borne out. First comes the witness in Jerusalem (Acts 2:47; 6:7), then Judea and Samaria (ch. 8:1), Galilee (chs. 9:31; 10:37), the extension to the " uttermost parts of the earth " (ch. 13:47), and the final opening of " a door of faith to the Gentiles " (ch. 14:27). To make certain that his audience doesn't miss the point, Luke occasionally repeats the " Jerusalem-Rome " motif (ch. 23:11), and brings down the curtain on the narrative with this closing speech by Paul:

> The Holy Spirit was right in saying to your fathers through Isaiah the prophet:
> " Go to this people, and say,
>   You shall indeed hear but never understand,
>   and you shall indeed see but never perceive. . . ."
> Let it be known to you then that this salvation of God has been sent to the Gentiles; they will listen.   (Ch. 28:25-26, 28.)

The journey is finished. Israel, Christ, and the Gentiles have each appeared in their own times. And Luke's theological point has been driven home: present time is the time of the Gentiles. Let us recognize this lest we be found " opposing God " (Acts 5:39).

In Defense of the Plan. Luke's contemporaries were not so credulous as to accept his " grand scheme " without batting a critical eyelash. In anticipation of their objections, Luke develops two wings of argumentation to defend his theory. The first might be called " proof from power "; the second, " proof from prophecy," a point that demands some slight additional examination.

Luke's " proof from power " draws its state's evidence from the life of Jesus and the current experience of the church. Pointing to the healings, " signs, and wonders " that emanate from both quarters (Luke 4:14, 36; 5:17; 6:19; 24:49; Acts 1:8), Luke adduces these as proofs or testimony of their divine origin. We see this in Peter's defense of Jesus before the Diaspora Jews in Jerusalem on the Day of Pentecost; Peter alludes to him as,

A man attested to you by God with mighty works and wonders and signs which God did through him in your midst. (Acts 2:22.)

Luke is the " spectacular " Gospel writer, appealing not so much to the ear as to the eye. Whereas in Mark, awe and amazement were signs of the absence of true faith, in Luke they are the only appropriate response. In order to evoke such a response from the " eye of faith," Luke even resorts to heightening the element of the miraculous. No story illustrates this Lucan propensity better than his version of the " call of the disciples." Whereas in Matthew and Mark (Matt. 4:18-22; Mark 1:16-20) the fishermen leave their nets and follow Jesus because of the *inherent* authority they sense in this man, in Luke (ch. 5:1-11), Peter follows Jesus only because Jesus was able to tell him where to make an incredible catch of fish. It is not the wisdom of God but the spectacle of God which Luke uses as his " proof from power," that God was in Israel, in Christ, and is now in the church.

Luke's "*proof from prophecy*," however, lies closest to his heart. In his special story about the rich man and Lazarus, Luke places a strange saying on the lips of Abraham. When the rich man urges Abraham to commission someone from the dead to inform his relatives of the torments of hell, Abraham says:

If they do not hear Moses and the prophets, neither will they be convinced if some one should rise from the dead. (Luke 16:31.)

What is implied in this admonition is the surprising contention that prophecy is of greater proof value than resurrection!

Luke's treatment of the resurrection story confirms the point. The significance of the resurrection, in Luke, is not the resurrection itself but the substantiating proof it supplies for the predictions or prophecies Jesus made during his lifetime that he would rise on the third day (Luke 9:22; 17:25). The whole of the narrative in Luke, ch. 24, consistently bears out this observation.

When Jesus accompanies the two Christians on the road to Emmaus, his business is to demonstrate, not that the Christ has risen, but, rather, how everything that happened to him in the preceding week (including the resurrection) is consistent with " Moses and all the prophets " (ch. 24:27). Luke drives the point a bit farther by having the two men say, " Did not our hearts burn within us . . . while he *opened to us the scriptures?* " And again, when Jesus appears to the disciples he tells them:

These are my words which I spoke to you, . . . that everything written about me in the law of Moses and the prophets and the psalms must be fulfilled. . . . Thus it is written, that the Christ should suffer and on the third day rise from the dead, and that repentance and forgiveness of sins should be preached in his name to all nations, beginning from Jerusalem. You are witnesses of these things. And behold, I send the promise of my Father upon

you; but stay in the city, until you are clothed with power from
on high. (Luke 24:44, 46-49.)

Luke uses the resurrection to establish the validity of proof
from prophecy. And he in turn uses proof from prophecy to
justify his whole scheme of history, from Moses, to Christ,
to the witness of the church before the Gentiles. As Paul
Schubert has suggested in his article " The Structure and
Significance of Luke 24," [20] proof from prophecy may be the
major theological thread running through Luke-Acts.

In Defense of the Faith. When Paul reaches Rome, one of
the first questions he faces is:

We desire to hear from you what your views are; for with regard to this sect we know that everywhere it is spoken against.
(Acts 28:22.)

A major part of Luke's task is to answer this question for
his own immediate audience. Surrounded by a relatively sus-
picious company of Jews and Romans, Luke takes the offensive in dispelling the myth of the contrariness of Christianity.

Addressing *the Judaic wing* of his critics, Luke attempts
to quiet their uneasiness over Christendom by assuring them
of the thorough Jewishness of all the major characters in the
story of Christianity. From John the Baptist, to Mary, to
Jesus, to Paul, they all walk " in all the commandments and
ordinances of the Lord blameless " (Luke 1:6). To prove
the point, he reminds his readers that both Jesus and John
were circumcised; their parents were devoted to the Temple;
Jesus frequently attended synagogue and made public readings from the Torah; the Christian church still observes the
Jewish Feast of Pentecost; Paul lives in " observance of the
law " (Acts 21:17-24), and on one occasion he hastened
from Miletus to Jerusalem in order to attend a Jewish festi-
val (ch. 20:16). If anyone is to be criticized, it is not the

Christians, argues Luke, but those false Jews, the " lawless " ones (ch. 2:23), who like their fathers insist on persecuting the prophets and emissaries of God (ch. 7:51-53).

Addressing *the Roman wing* of his critics, Luke faces an imposing criticism. Official Rome eyes Christianity with justifiable suspicion; its leader and founder was executed under capital Roman law, and many of its protagonists, such as Peter, Paul, and Silas, have been under Roman arrest on more than one occasion. Over against growing suspicion that Christianity is nothing more than a rabble-rousing sect, Luke builds up an impressive defense. The first premise of the defense is similar to his apologetic to the Jews, namely, that Jerusalem Jewry and its vindictiveness is responsible for Christian incarceration. But the second premise deals with a " fact " Luke repeats again and again in various disguises, that no Roman court has ever found a Christian guilty.

The legal innocence of Christianity is a major Lucan theme. In Jesus' trial before Pilate, not once, but three times, Pilate declares, " I find no crime in this man " (Luke 23:4, 14-15, 22; cf. Acts 13:28), and only because " their voices prevailed " (Luke 23:23) does Pilate grant the option of choosing between Barabbas and Jesus. If the Roman reader misses the point in the trial scene, Luke reinforces it at the crucifixion where one of the malefactors who was crucified with Jesus tells the other, " This man has done nothing wrong " (v. 41). The epitome of the argument occurs at the moment Jesus dies; note Luke's editing of the centurion's confession:

Matt. 27:54	Mark 15:39	Luke 23:47
Truly this was a son of God!	Truly this man was a son of God!	Certainly this man was innocent!

In like fashion in The Acts, Paul is publicly acquitted by his Roman judges, Claudius Lysias the Jerusalem tribune

(Acts 23:29), Porcius Festus the Governor of Caesarea (ch. 25:18, 25), and King Agrippa (ch. 26:31). Speaking for Christianity as a whole, Luke writes these words:

Neither against the law of the Jews, nor against the temple, nor against Caesar have I offended at all. (Acts 25:8.)

The theological point hidden in Luke's public defense against Jewish and Roman criticism is that despite the malevolence of Jerusalem Jewry and the " accidental " injustice of Roman law, neither Christ nor Christianity was stifled. Why? Because — and this is the point of the argument — they are part of God's plan, which is preferential to neither Jews nor Romans, but is intended for the salvation of both.

A God-centered Plan. All in all, the theme of Luke-Acts is that man's history is God's history. Man and beast, Jew and Roman, Savior and the saved, are all parts of a historical whole created and guided by God:

The God who made the world and everything in it, being Lord of heaven and earth, does not live in shrines made by man, nor is he served by human hands, as though he needed anything, since he himself gives to all men life and breath and everything . . . for
' In him we live and move and have our being.' "
(Acts 17:24-25, 28.)

Luke is the God-intoxicated Evangelist. Though statistics may be deceiving, we cannot help being impressed by the fact that, whereas the name " God " appears in Matthew only 55 times, in Mark 52 times, and in John 84 times, it occurs in Luke *124 times* and in Acts *172 times*.

God alone is the central actor in history. When blind Bartimaeus receives his sight, it is God who is glorified (Luke 18:43; cf. Mark 10:52; Matt. 20:34). When the centurion observes Jesus' death, it is God who is praised (Luke

23:47). And when Jesus enters Jerusalem on the colt, Luke tells us, " The whole multitude of the disciples began to rejoice and praise God with a loud voice for all the mighty works that they had seen " (ch. 19:37).

The line between theology and Christology, between God and Christ, is essential to Luke's theology of history. Jesus, though the center of history, is always subordinate to the God of history. This fact comes out in subtle ways, for example, in this comparison:

Mark 1:38	Luke 4:43
Let us go on to the next towns, that I may preach there also; for *that is why I came out.*	I must preach the good news . . . to the other cities also; for *I was sent* for this purpose.

The Jesus who acts on his own in Mark is clearly under divine commission in Luke. Jesus is praised, not for himself, but because he is *God's* Messiah (Luke 9:20). It is *God* who anoints Jesus with the Holy Spirit and with power (Acts 10:36-37). Even the birth stories in Luke, chs. 1 and 2, redound to the glories of God rather than to the glory of the child; Zechariah, Mary, the angels, the shepherds, and the aged Simeon all give glory to " God in the highest " (chs. 1:32, 35, 76; 2:14; 6:35; Acts 7:48; 16:17), as he who has " visited and redeemed his people " (Luke 1:68). For Luke, God is the eternal subject of history and Christ is a moment in his self-revelation. The fine balance between the two is deftly expressed by the crowd at the raising of the widow's son at Nain (Luke 7:16):

Fear seized them all; and they glorified God, saying, " A great prophet has arisen among us! " and " God has visited his people! "

CHRIST AND SALVATION: ESSENCE AND EXISTENCE

The angel's proclamation to the shepherds who watched over their flock by night captures the substance and the ambiguity of Luke's Christology:

For to you is born this day in the city of David a Savior, who is Christ the Lord. (Luke 2:11.)

The careful juxtaposition of the three titles, Savior, Christ, and Lord, expresses quite succinctly Luke's formulation and solution of a perennial Christological problem. For Luke, the term " Savior " sums up his personal evaluation of Jesus' relevance for human *existence;* whereas the terms " Christ " and " Lord " express his evaluation of Jesus' place in the world of men and of the gods, his divine *essence.*

Christ and Lord: Jesus in Essence. The problem of Christological " essence " or identity will continue to be an issue as long as the church keeps its " head," since the problem is fundamentally an intellectual one. It seeks to answer the question of Jesus' place in the divine-human spectrum, his relation to past and future religious phenomena, and his position with respect to the present community that bears his name.

In his concern to solve the question, not only for himself but for his friends and opponents, Luke proposes a selection of titles, some of which he personally emphasizes, and others which he simply draws from the currently meaningful vocabulary of the church.

Although Luke employs the term *Christ* because of its Messianic " proof value " among a Jewish audience (Luke 24:26, 45 f.; Acts 17:3; 18:5; 26:22), in general he tends to disuse it because it carries little, if any, meaning for a thoroughly Greek audience. In deference to the Greek mind,

Luke tends to employ other Christological terms more immediately intelligible to it, for example, "Son of the Most High" (Luke 1:32), "Son of God" (ch. 22:70), "servant" (Acts 3:13, 26; 4:27, 30), and "prophet" (Luke 7:16, 39; 9:8, 19; 24:19) — all of which bear a negotiable meaning in the Hellenistic as well as the Jewish context.

The gem in Luke's Christological treasury is the term *Lord* (Greek, *kyrios*). Luke uses *kyrios* with greater frequency than any other Gospel writer. We can attribute his fascination with the term to the fact that it carries a wealth of meaning in *both* the religious worlds that Luke hopes to reach, the Judaic and the Greek.

For the Diaspora Jew, who speaks Greek but does his religious thinking in Old Testament terms, the title *kyrios* is eminently familiar as the Greek translation of Yahweh or Jehovah. For the Greek, on the other hand, the title *kyrios* is thoroughly familiar, first, as a cult name in emperor worship, applied to Caligula, Claudius, and Nero; second, as a title in the popular and numerous "mystery cults," whose deities, Osiris, Serapis, and Hermes-Thoth, are commonly addressed in worship as "Lord." Thus, as Luke fully recognizes, for the Jew, the term *kyrios* evokes the image of the creator of the world and the ruler of history; for the Greek, it implies one who has conquered death and made his sovereign presence felt in the cult. With all of its meanings, the title *kyrios* faithfully communicates Luke's conception of the essence or identity of Jesus vis-à-vis God and the community of Christians.

The Savior: Jesus for Existence. Although the expression "Jesus saves" has acquired a legacy of misinterpretation in our own time, it sums up the meaning of Christianity in most of its history, because the term "save" or "salvation" in its Hebrew, Greek, and even Latin forms, always means "to

make whole," " to create health," " to heal." This connotation can be seen in Acts 27:34, where the Greek word
sōtēria, elsewhere translated " salvation," here is translated
as that physical "strength " or " health " which comes to a
hungry man when he takes food again. Though we cannot
know whether Luke is a professional " healer," it is clear
that he has a personal interest in it, as is evidenced in the
fact that he is the only Gospel maker to use the terms
" Savior " (*sōtēr*) and " salvation " (*sōtēria* and *sōtērion*),
with the one exception of a single verse in John (ch. 4:22).

The Gospel of Luke is a Gospel of healing and salvation.
Jesus begins his ministry in Luke on this note (Luke 4:18-
19) and Paul ends with this note (Acts 28:28). Although the
term probably has implications for the future life, Luke
tends to use " salvation " in a this-worldly sense, referring
to three types: physical, spiritual, and social.

Physical salvation in Luke refers to the numerous acts of
healing " the poor, the maimed, the lame, the blind " (Luke
14:13, 21) performed both by Jesus and by the early church.
It is the "perfect health" of which Peter speaks in Acts
3:16, and it is also involvement with the plight of the poor.
The poor occupy a special place in Luke's Gospel. He cites
Jesus' praise of Zacchaeus for his generosity toward the poor
(Luke 6:20, 24); he emphasizes the distinction between a
man who has " true riches " (ch. 16:11) and one who is
" not rich toward God " (ch. 12:21); and he describes
the experimental community in Jerusalem as one in which
" there was not a needy person among them, for as many as
were possessors of lands or houses sold them . . . and dis-
tribution was made to each as any had need " (Acts 4:34-
35). This excessive concern for the physical state of man,
apparent in both volumes, may even provide substantiation
of the thesis that Luke is the physician-companion of Paul
(Col. 4:14; II Tim. 4:11; Philemon 24).

Spiritual salvation consists in "repentance" and "forgiveness." As we discover also in Mark, the radically sick man is the man who knows no forgiveness. One of the most remarkable dramatizations of this is found in Luke's version of the story about the "woman of the city" who washes Jesus' feet with her tears. In Luke, this story climaxes with the epigrammatic statement (ch. 7:47):

Therefore I tell you, her sins, which are many, are forgiven, for she loved much; but he who is forgiven little, loves little.

Luke understands Jesus to be saying that the capacity to love presupposes the capacity to be forgiven. This may account for Luke's continuing interest in forgiveness, as highlighted in the classic Lucan parables of the lost sheep, the lost coin, and the prodigal son (Luke, ch. 15): "There will be more joy in heaven over one sinner who repents than over ninety-nine righteous persons who need no repentance."

What is repentance? For Luke, as for Mark, repentance involves a reorientation of the self, the mind, the heart, and the spirit. It means moving from "sin," which is basically "ignorance" of God (Acts 3:17; 13:27), to forgiveness, which is an open acceptance of God. Repentance involves trusting in God's righteousness rather than one's own (Luke 18:9-14); seeking God's plan rather than one's own (Acts 5:39). In summary, repentance means welcoming the salvation that God has manifested first in Israel, second, in Christ, and now in the Spirit that is abroad in the church (Acts 16:17).

Social salvation comes as an antidote to human "apartness." Luke, the universal thinker, appears to be profoundly disturbed at the walls of division between the rich and the poor, the religious outcast and the Pharisee, the Judean and the Samaritan, the male and the female, the Jew and the Gentile. A kind of ecumenist, Luke is dedicated to "heal-

ing " the divisions in society, as is apparent in his concern
with the outcast and the non-Judean; in his involvement
with the inclusion of women into the ranks of Christianity —
many of whom he mentions by name, Mary Magdalene,
Joanna, Dorcas, Lydia, and the like; it appears most obviously in his concern to extend the " salvation of God " to the
Gentiles. As Luke says in a hundred different ways, the " salvation " that comes through Christ is " prepared in the
presence of *all* peoples "; it is not a salvation for the elite
(Luke 2:32).

In hailing Jesus as " Savior," Luke is declaring him as a
rival to the succession of Roman emperors who were also
addressed as *sōtēr*. For Luke, Jesus is the new ruler who
brings a salvation that no temporal ruler can know, and who
sustains his people, not with a *pax Romana,* but with the
pax spiritus.

The Spirit and the Church: A Sacramental Theology

Underlying Luke's interpretation of history and his evaluation of Jesus as Savior and Lord is a sacramental concept
of the world. The catechism definition of sacrament is, " a
visible expression of an invisible grace," which is a theo-
logically versed way of saying that God manifests himself
through *natural* forms.

Taken in this sense, the word " sacramental " applies to
Luke's theology. For as we enter Luke's world, we begin to
perceive an extremely vital, progressive, contemporary theological perspective which is never surprised at the new forms
God chooses for his self-expression: a dove, a child in a
manger, a tongue of fire. Psychologically opposed to orthodoxy, Luke is the perennially liberal theologian who has his
theological antennae prepared for any wavelength on which

God might choose to speak. God has appeared through the prophets and priests of Israel; but, Luke insists, we dare not rest content with that. God has also appeared in Christ and his disciples; but, Luke proposes, this is not all we can expect to hear from him. For even now, Luke tells us, God is appearing in manifold forms (Acts 26:15-17) in the midst of the church.

The recognition of the Spirit's presence in the church constitutes both the major premise and problem of Luke's writing. Through his Gospel and his book of " acts," Luke hopes to answer at least this one question: How does the church, as a " sacramental reality," relate to the world? He answers it with at least three separate observations.

First, Luke proposes that the church is to be *a medium of ministering fellowship rather than a haven of self-saving individualists*. Even though Luke speaks of ecclesiastical officialdom more than any other Gospel does, he shows a remarkable disdain for " rank " (Acts, ch. 15) and a remarkable insistence on the mutual responsibility of all Christians, both those with special gifts and those without.

The Lucan emphasis is on service or " ministry " (Greek, *diakonia;* cf. Acts 1:17, 25; 6:1, 4; 11:29; 12:25; 20:24; 21:19) in which each member determines, " every one according to his *diakonia*," his " service-ability," " to send relief to the brethren " (Acts 11:29). Regardless of one's position as " guardian " (*episkopos*), " deacon," or " elder," one is to keep Christ as his model: " I am among you as one who serves " (Luke 22:27). For Luke, no Christian can be an " island unto himself "; he must always be a conscious part of the interlocking landmass of humanity.

Second, Luke affirms that the constant element in the church is its *spiritual rather than geographical orientation*. The sanctifying element in the New Israel is not its " sacred space," such as Jerusalem, the " place " in which it is rooted, but its Holy Spirit, the " force " by which it is vitalized. In one of his highway signs in The Acts (ch. 9:31), Luke tells us:

So the church throughout all Judea and Galilee and Samaria had peace and was built up; and walking in the fear of the Lord and in the comfort of the Holy Spirit it was multiplied.

The church is where the Spirit is. And, we must add, the Spirit is wherever praying Christians are.

Prayer is a major focal point in Luke. He tells us that Jesus relied on prayer constantly — on one occasion, all night (Luke 6:12); he shows us how the disciples were instructed in prayer (Luke 11:2-4); every prominent figure in The Acts, from Peter to Paul, constantly depends upon prayer for his wholeness. Three of the most provocative parables in Luke are designed to illumine its meaning: the story of the friend who nags his neighbor for bread at midnight until the neighbor concedes (ch. 11:5-8); the tale of the widow who camps on the judge's conscience until he submits to hearing her out (ch. 18:1-8); and the shaded comparison between the publican and his simple utterance, and the Pharisee, with his unconsciously audacious boast (vs. 9-14). Prayer is the sacramental experience, for Luke. Formal or informal, communal or individual, anguished or joyful, it is the means by which the man who seeks God is found by him. The center of Christian living is neither Jerusalem, nor Antioch, nor Rome, but life in consciousness of the Spirit — which is prayer.

Third, perhaps the trademark of Luke's ecclesiology is his emphasis that the church be *an exoteric rather than esoteric medium of the Spirit,* directed toward the world, not away from it. With the idealism of the World Council of Churches, the universal humanitarianism of UNICEF, and the evangelical zeal of the Voice of America, Luke spreads out his theological net to catch men of every shape, color, and intellectual persuasion. He gathers Ethiopian eunuchs, Roman centurions, Thyatiran dyers, Rabbinic students, and Galilean fishermen into the picture. His armory of words is loaded with the verbs " to proclaim," " to announce," " to evangelize," " to pronounce," et cetera; and his preaching itinerary stretches to the "end of the earth." Perhaps more than any other Gospel, Luke has inspired Christianity out of the catacomb and into the world, with the affirmation that it is in the world that God's presence and God's work are to be discovered.

History, Theology, and Aesthetics

Why did Luke write? Not because history stood there like Mount Everest and had to be mastered. He wrote under the same compulsion that drove Einstein to publish his famous equations, Bach to produce his Masses, and Van Gogh to plant olive groves and cherry trees on canvas. Luke had a vision, an idea, a concept of reality, that had to break into words. Not only was the idea ingenious; it was beautiful.

Luke can scarcely conceal his passion for beauty. His double volume exudes the beauty of the well-turned phrase and the polished narrative. B. H. Streeter recognized this in saluting Luke as " a consummate literary artist," as did oft-quoted Ernst Renan when he hailed Luke as " the most beautiful book in the world." The rich vegetation of poetry in the birth stories, preserved in our literature and music as the Magnificat and the Nunc Dimittis; the finely wrought portraits of Zechariah and of the youthful Mary; the polished revisions of such parables as the mustard seed; and the dramatically astute introductions of Pilate and the high priest Caiaphas long before they assume important roles in the narrative — all these are marks of a skilled pen, but also of a mind that is tuned to the aesthetic.

Romano Guardini,[21] a Roman Catholic theologian of acknowledged stature in Roman and Protestant circles, once wrote this observation on Dostoevsky's idea of beauty as it emerges in *The Brothers Karamazov:*

In the words of Zossima, beauty is not only the supreme concept of all values, but something which includes the true and the good, something that " people are thirsty to receive."

Luke's passion for beauty is unsated by the mere opportunity to write well. It is seeing, beholding the beautiful that feeds his soul. And as Guardini comments, the beautiful for Luke is tantamount to the good and the true.

The beautiful and the good is a formulation worked out in Platonic philosophy. For Plato, the highest Idea was the Good. For Luke, also, the highest beauty is the good, in a humanitarian sense. It was probably less than accidental that Luke sought to capture the good news he associated with Jesus in poetry rather than in prose, as he introduces Jesus' mission to his readers (Luke 4:18 f.). In terms of Luke's perception, the good news to the poor, the release to the captives, and the recovering of sight to the blind enter into the realm of religious aesthetics. They are touched with a " divine beauty."

The beautiful and the true might be equated in Luke with the beautiful and the symmetrical. There is a touch of the mathematician or the logician in Luke. What pleases him about his vision of history is not only its relevance to man; there is an architectural splendor and marvel of symmetry to the plan that evokes an aesthetic response. In many ways Luke recalls the aesthetic jubilance of the psalmist as he beholds the structure of the cosmos:

> The heavens declare the glory of God;
> And the firmament showeth his handiwork.
>   (Ps. 19:1, KJV.)

It seems likely that Luke may have been one of those hundreds of " God-fearers " in the Greco-Roman world of whom F. C. Grant tells us in his *Roman Hellenism and the New Testament:* [22]

[They] discovered the Jewish Bible, in the Greek translation, and found themselves irresistibly drawn to the Jewish synagogue with its noble ethics, its spiritual conception of the supreme Being, its positive revelation of God's requirements, and its deeply ingrained eschatology, its conviction of a divine purpose running through all of life and a definite goal toward which history is moving.

As a converted Jew and Christian, Luke has stumbled into the open space of a world the vastness and beauty of which is so overwhelming for him that he is forced to give it expression.

Theology and aesthetics are nearly synonymous for this Grecian-Jewish-Christian mind who sees more occasions for joy than for suffering in his world. Perhaps he was, as many have observed, somewhat deficient in his ability to see the multiple significance and possibility in suffering, in the same perceptive way Mark does. Nevertheless, Luke has an abundance of joy that offers ample and perhaps happily corrective compensation. Luke's joy is not of the apocalyptic genre that derives from the thought of having one foot in heaven, which means having only one left to remove from the earth. Luke's joy is this-worldly, rooted in what God has done and is doing on earth, from the " tidings of great joy " that accompany the birth of Jesus, to the return of the disciples to Jerusalem " with great joy " to await the power from on high (Luke 24:52). Luke is a Gospel conceived and born in theological, historical, and religiously aesthetic joy.

34b 75

V THE GOSPEL OF JOHN:
A Paradoxical-Mystical Approach

THE *Mona Lisa* and the Fourth Gospel share two artistic qualities, beauty and enigma. Certainly, it is the spiritual allurement of this Gospel that makes it the favorite of Protestants, Catholics, and Christian Scientists alike. Yet what its beauty achieves in the way of ecumenical concord, its enigmatic visage threatens to disrupt.

John probably ranks as the most controversial of the Gospels. Mark, Matthew, and Luke have an ordinary siege of critical afflictions, but John represents a veritable epidemic. Is he a Gnostic Jew, an Alexandrian Jew, a Hellenist, or a Palestinian? Did he write very late, after A.D. 100, as scholars have thought for years, or was he the earliest Gospel writer as his affinities with Qumrân dualistic thinking may suggest? Who was the author who identifies himself solely as the " beloved disciple "? Was he John the son of Zebedee, or John Mark the companion of Paul, or Lazarus — as Floyd Filson has recently suggested; or was he an unknown Christian Gnostic writing under an apostolic pseudonym? By no means the least of the problems is whether John was written by one, two, or three different hands! Most scholars agree that ch. 21 is an addendum tacked on to an original ending still visible in ch. 20:30-31. And some insist, with F. C. Grant, that John is a " seamless robe."

Not all these questions are totally insoluble. In the light of recent scholarship, especially J. A. T. Robinson's " The Destination and Purpose of St. John's Gospel," [23] it seems likely that John is a Jew writing to Jews about Jews. John's thesis, so familiar from Paul and Matthew, is that one can be a true Jew and a Christian at the same time. His audience consists of Greek Jews of the Diaspora ("the Greeks," John 7:35; 12:20), to whom he is issuing the complaint that the Judean Jews (the " Jews ") have, in obdurate ignorance, crucified the very Messiah that Moses foretold (ch. 5:38-46). The point of the argument is that the " Greeks " must beware of making the same erroneous judgment.

John is waging war on two other fronts as well, against the Docetics, who allege that Jesus is true spirit but not the flesh (cf. chs. 1:14; 19:34), and against the John the Baptist party, who hold that John the Baptist rather than Jesus is the Messiah (cf. chs. 1:6-8, 19-34; 3:22-30). Though on the surface the writer of a " spiritual Gospel," John is not beyond rolling up his shirt sleeves to engage in practical matters. He stands about somewhat like a doting parent inserting editorial comment after editorial comment, either translating Hebrew terms (chs. 1:38, 41-42; 4:9, 25; 5:2; 20:16), or " explaining " why Jesus, Judas, or the Pharisees acted and thought the way they did (cf. chs. 6:64; 7:39; 8:13; 12:6, 33; 13:11; 21:19), or on one occasion explaining why Isaiah indulged in one of his prophecies (ch. 12:41; Isa. 6:10).

Although a vague resemblance exists between John and the Synoptics, the similarity is in all likelihood due to common oral tradition rather than to direct borrowing. The contrast between the long discourses in John and the clipped parables in the Synoptics, and the absence of the baptism narrative, of exorcism accounts, and of references to the Kingdom of God, so prominent in Matthew, Mark, and Luke, lead to the conclusion that John is a " first " Gospel in the same way Mark is. John is starting afresh, working with a basketful of random traditions about Jesus, possibly personal recollections, but above all, with a clearly defined vision in his head. It may even be that John is " the " first rather than last Gospel, as has often been suggested.

One notable parallel with the Synoptic Gospels is apparent in the structural similarity between John and Mark. Both divide their Gospels into balanced halves. In the first twelve chapters of John, Jesus' ministry is the subject; he addresses the crowds; his " hour has not yet come " (chs. 2:4; 7:6, 30; 8:20); he performs " signs "; and finally, Lazarus, a friend of Jesus', dies and is raised (ch. 11). In the second half, chapters 13 to 20, Jesus' crucifixion and departure provide the theme, and the situation reverses. Jesus now directs his discourses to the disciples rather than to the crowds; he speaks " openly " (ch. 18:20) rather than in figures (ch. 16:25-33); his hour comes (chs. 12:23; 13:1; 17:1); he performs no more " signs "; and finally he dies and is raised. Whether this remarkable affinity with Mark is grounds for establishing literary dependence remains a moot question. However, little substantial similarity exists beyond this one striking parallel.

Despite the meager certainties that Johannine scholarship has been able to uncover, and despite the jigsaw patterns in the varied solutions they have offered, one still senses a fundamental and pervasive unity in the spirit and temperament of the Gospel itself. Even if two or three editorial voices are speaking in John, they appear to be chanting in a unified, harmonic pattern. Although this pattern defies precise definition, and although its relation to Synoptic patterns is nebulous, its controlling motifs can be described. Two of these are mysticism and paradox.

MYSTICISM AND PARADOX

Rudolf Bultmann, frequently acknowledged as the *maior domus* among Johannine commentators, refuses to join in dubbing John as a " mystical " Gospel, contending that John lacks that zest for disciplining the soul and cultivating " religious experiences " so characteristic of classical mysticism. If we were to accept Bultmann's highly specialized and minimal definition of mysticism, we would have to agree that the term cannot be applied to John. But if we were to use " mysticism " in the broader sense in which it is customarily applied to such figures as Paul, William Wordsworth, George Fox, Meister Eckhardt, and even Jesus of Nazareth, we would find that John clearly belongs to the " mystical " category.

The term " mystical " embraces those attitudes which characterize an intuitive, quasi-otherworldly approach to reality. John Wright Buckham [24] has listed seven such attitudes characteristic of the mystical approach: (1) seeking the reality within; (2) seeking the meaning in mystery; (3) seeking the eternal in the temporal; (4) seeking the solitude that leads to spiritual growth; (5) seeking occasions for service; (6) seeking humility; (7) seeking a love that participates in the divine love. The famous prayer of St. Francis, the *De Imitatione Christi* of Thomas à Kempis, *The City of God* of St. Augustine, perhaps even the *Symposium* of Plato, seem to capture the essence of this description, as also does the Fourth Gospel with its emphasis on spiritual rebirth (ch. 3:5), on living water (ch. 4:10), on the necessity for love (ch. 14), and on the oneness that unites God and man (ch. 17). In his classical *Systematic Theology*,[25] Paul Tillich offers this definition of the mystical:

" Mystical " is . . . a category which characterizes the divine as being present in experience. In this sense, the mystical is the heart of every religion as religion. . . . Mysticism [presupposes] the experience of ultimacy in being and meaning.

The term " paradoxical " also applies to the Fourth Gospel. The subject of the Fourth Gospel, as John conceives of it, lends itself quite naturally to paradoxical description. On the one hand, it is otherworldly, transcendent, spiritual, and eternal; on the other hand, it is this-worldly in its concerns, immanent, involved with the flesh, and relevant for human history. John's way of viewing his subject may be the source of the apparent conflict; for he views it both from the classical Greek perspective which approaches reality in static, metaphysical, eternal, and spatial terms, and from the classical Hebraic perspective which approaches reality in dynamic, practical, temporal, and historical terms. John appears to be viewing reality from both vantage points. The only means open to him for describing his two-dimensional experience is the device of *paradox*, either as an intentional or, possibly, as an unconscious device.

Literally, *paradox* means " contrary to opinion," the point being that a paradox is complete when two statements that " appear " to contradict each other are made with equal vehemence. The theologian, the poet, the philosopher, the politician, but at times even the physicist and the physician, are frequently given to paradoxical expression. When the theologian affirms that " God acts in history," he almost always adds, " But of course, God is also transcendent to history," in much the same way the atomic physicist is apt to waver between discussions of the velocity and mass of nuclear particles, or in the way a physician will stand between the known and unknown factors in a diagnosis.

John is inclined to speak in both paradoxical and mystical terms. Whether by direct intention or by inclination, we cannot know. We can only observe the fact that he does. His language, and presumably his conscious intellect, focuses on that fine line between externals and internals, between the obvious and the subtle, the visible and the hidden. In many respects all theological language tries to focus in this area. And it may be that the paradoxical-mystical tongue John speaks is the authentic lingua franca of the complete theologian in any age.

CHRISTOLOGY AND PARADOX

The Christ of the Fourth Gospel bears only slight literal resemblance to the Christ of the Synoptics. Though the traditional Synoptic titles, Master, Christ, Lord, Savior, et cetera, appear in this Gospel, they fail to relate to the peculiar vitality of the Johannine portrait. John presents his readers with an original range of natural symbols which have become the distinctive marks of Johannine Christology: the bread of life, the light of the world, living water, the way, the truth, the life, the resurrection, the true vine.

However, John not only relies on a new set of symbols to communicate his conception of Christ, he also employs a paradoxical method of Christological description. Rather than stating who Jesus is and whence he comes, in a statistical, biographical sense, John chooses to put paradoxical Christological statements on the lips of the dramatis personae in the Gospel. From them we are led to discover three propositions: first, that Jesus is out of this world and opposed to the world, and yet *in* the world and *for* the world; second, that he is one with the Father, and yet distinct from him; third, that he reveals the truth, but that this truth is not a fact but a living reality.

Christ and the World. The author of the Fourth Gospel stands on a Dali-esque inclined plane that ascends in one direction into infinite light and that descends in the other into darkness. John depicts himself and the whole of humanity as standing on the dark half of the continuum pondering whether to remain in darkness or turn toward the light. The darkness is called *kosmos*, " the world "; the light is *theos*, God.

The dramatic dialogue between " this world " and the " other " is sustained by a rich fabric of contradictory images, designed to capture the reality which John senses so powerfully, that man does in fact live between life and death, between good and evil, between possibility and destruction. One cannot turn a page in the Fourth Gospel without coming across a new set of these religious dualistic images: light vs. darkness (chs. 1:1 ff.; 8:12; 12:35-36); rebirth vs. natural birth (chs. 3:6; 16:21); spirit vs. flesh (chs. 3:6; 6:63; 1:13); living water vs. natural water (chs. 4:10; 7:38); worship in spirit and truth vs. worship in temples (ch. 4:23 ff.); the bread of heaven vs. ordinary bread (chs. 4:31; 6:32); the day vs. the night (chs. 9:4; 11:9-10; 13:30); the shepherd vs. the thief (ch. 10:1-18); life vs. death (ch. 11:25 ff.); peace vs. tribulation (ch. 16:33); joy vs. sorrow (ch. 16:21-24); the right vs. the wrong (ch. 18:23); and heavenly kingship vs. earthly kingship (ch. 18:36 ff.).

Although the *kosmos* represents the source of destruction, evil, and eternal death for John, it is not to be identified solely with the flesh and material existence. *Kosmos* is a paradoxical reality in John. Though all that is in the world is flesh, not all that is in the flesh is " worldly." Thus, *kosmos* is not a literal, but a metaphorical term, personifying all those forces *within the physical world* which oppose the light.

If the world hates you, know that it has hated me before it hated you. If you were of the world, the world would love its own; but because you are not of the world, but I chose you out of the world, therefore the world hates you. (Ch. 15:18-19; cf. ch. 17:14.)

John can speak of " his own " (ch. 13:1) as being *in* the *kosmos* but not lost (ch. 17:12); they are *in* the world as the Word also was *in* the world (chs. 1:10; 17:6-19), but they are not *of* the world. They are *in* the flesh, but are not born *of* the flesh, having been reborn of the Spirit of God (chs. 1:13; 3:6). The question, " To be or not to be " is not the choice between spirit and flesh, as such, but the choice between turning toward the *kosmos* as the ground of one's being or toward God, the true ground of being.

In the Fourth Gospel, Jesus is clothed in the mythological attire of the Savior (ch. 4:42) who comes from the realm of light to redeem " his own " from the darkness. He is " from heaven," addressing himself to those who are " of the earth " (ch. 3:27, 31). He comes from being with God (chs. 13:3; 16:30; 17:8) to be with man. He travels across the vast space between the realm of light and the realm of darkness:

You are from below, I am from above; you are of this world, I am not of this world. (Ch. 8:23.)

He is sent because God loves the world (ch. 3:16). His mission is to bear light into the darkness of the world, and so effect a release from enslavement to darkness. Once having accomplished this, he will return " to the Father " (chs. 14:28; 16:10, 17, 28; 17:11, 13) to prepare a place for those whom the father has given him from out of the world (chs. 14:1-4; 17:6-19).

With this strange mythological imagery, John is portraying the Christian experience of the light that has come into the darkness of the world in the person of Jesus. To say that Jesus is " the light of the world " (ch. 9:5) is almost a literal truth for John. Poignantly aware of the dimensions of darkness in the structure of reality, John's Gospel proclaims that " this-worldliness " is tolerable only in the light that comes from the " other," that life *in* the *kosmos* has hope

only if one realizes that though one is *in* the *kosmos,* one is
not *of* the *kosmos* (ch. 17:16). John is neither " this-
worldly " nor " otherworldly "; he appears to be both.

Christ the Logos. The Christology of the Fourth Gospel
seesaws between two sets of affirmations: first, that " I and
the Father are one " (ch. 10:30); second, that " the Father
is greater than I " (ch. 14:28). The fulcrum of the seesaw
is the Johannine doctrine of the Logos.

The first set of affirmations dealing with the oneness of
Jesus and God invariably focuses on the " I " of Jesus. " I "
(*ego*) appears 142 times in John as opposed to 31 times in
Matthew, 18 in Mark, and 23 in Luke. Frequently the " I "
is set in the famous Johannine I AM sayings:

6:35,48,51	" I AM the bread of life " (or " living bread ")
6:41	" I AM the bread which came down from heaven "
8:12	" I AM the light of the world "
8:18	" I AM he who witnesses to myself "
8:23	" I AM from above "
8:23	" I AM not of this world "
10:7,9	" I AM the door of the sheep "
10:11,14	" I AM the good shepherd "
11:25	" I AM the resurrection and the life "
14:6	" I AM the way, and the truth, and the life "
15:1,5	" I AM the true vine "

On several occasions the I AM appears with no predicate
nominative. When the woman at the well informs Jesus that
the Messiah is to reveal all things, Jesus replies, " I AM [he]
who speaks to you " (ch. 4:26). Likewise, as Jesus walks on
the sea he reassures the frightened disciples: " I AM; do not
be afraid " (ch. 6:20). To the crowds he announces: " When
you have lifted up the Son of man, then you will know that
I AM . . ." (ch. 8:28), and later, " Truly, truly, I say to
you, before Abraham was, I AM " (v. 58). Perhaps the most
obvious exposure of John's I AM theology appears in the

betrayal scene. As the soldiers and priests approach Jesus in
the Garden with lanterns and torches, John tells us:

> Then Jesus . . . said to them, " Whom do you seek? " They
> answered him, " Jesus of Nazareth." Jesus said to them, " *I AM*
> [he]." Judas, who betrayed him, was standing with them. When he
> said to them, " *I AM* [he]," they drew back and fell to the ground.
> Again he asked them, " Whom do you seek? " And they said,
> " Jesus of Nazareth." Jesus answered, " I told you that *I AM*
> [he]." (Ch. 18:4-8.)

The I AM is, as noted earlier, a Hellenistic-Judaic symbol
for deity. The point of its use here is to provide a qualitative
identification of Jesus with God. Through this symbol, John
is expressing in his own way what Christianity has affirmed
from the beginning, that to confront Jesus is to confront the
power of God. To put it in the prosaic words of Nicodemus,
rather than in poetic-symbolic language:

> Rabbi, we know that you are a teacher come from God; for no
> one can do these signs that you do, unless God is with him. (Ch.
> 3:2.)

The second set of affirmations, completing the paradox,
baldly denies the absolute identity of Jesus and the I AM.
Whereas sovereign self-confidence is the motif in the first
set, self-effacement and humility constitute the theme of the
second:

> Truly, truly, I say to you, the Son can do nothing of his own
> accord, but only what he sees the Father doing. . . . I can do
> nothing on my own authority; as I hear, I judge; and my judg-
> ment is just, because I seek not my own will but the will of him
> who sent me. If I bear witness to myself, my testimony is not true.
> (Ch. 5:19, 30-31.)

Throughout these sayings, Jesus professes that he has been
sent. He is not doing his own will but the will of him who sent
him (chs. 6:38; 14:24). His teaching belongs to the one who

sent him (ch. 7:16). If a man believes in him, sees him, or receives him, he believes, sees, and receives *not* him, but the one who sent him (chs. 12:44-45; 13:16). Jesus is a man on a mission; an emissary of the truth (ch. 18:37). His goal is to complete (*teleioun*) the work God has given him (chs. 4:34; 5:36; 17:4). John self-consciously underlines this mission in final words, which Jesus utters on the cross: " It is finished " (ch. 19:30; Greek, *tetelestai,* " It has been completed ").

The fulcrum that holds these pro-I AM and anti-I AM affirmations in meaningful counterbalance is the Johannine doctrine of the *logos.* Were a Greek-speaking Hebrew to read the Prologue to the Fourth Gospel, " In the beginning was the *Logos,* . . ." he would understand its significance instantaneously; whereas a modern reader finds it necessary to puzzle over it. Both in Hebraic and Hellenistic culture the term *logos* (or Hebrew, *dabar*) meant that " word " or " self-expression " by which a man, or God, makes himself known. The language of Plato expresses this idea quite clearly. Plato speaks of two *logoi* in man (or God): the *logos* in the mind, the " thought " *logos,* and the *logos* of the tongue, the spoken *logos.* He illustrates this in human experience. As a man is unknown until he speaks or enacts his *logos,* so God is unknown until he utters his *logos* to man. In the Prologue to John, we find this precise idea. The *logos* was originally with God in the mind of God, so to speak, indeed, *was* God (ch. 1:1). However, the *logos* or " inner thought " of God did not remain hidden; " the *logos* became flesh and dwelt among us " (v. 14). For those who may have missed the point, John concludes his Prologue with this direct translation of the idea:

No one has ever seen God; the only Son, who is in the bosom of the Father, he has made him known. (Ch. 1:18.)

Jesus both is and is not God. He is God's *logos*.

Christ and Revelation. Though " revelation " never appears as a " term " in the vocabulary of the Fourth Gospel, it remains its central theme. Rudolf Bultmann describes the Johannine conception of revelation with this cryptic but penetrating comment: [26]

> Jesus, as the Revealer of God, reveals nothing but that he is the Revealer. . . . John . . . in his Gospel presents only the fact (*das Dass*) of the Revelation without describing its content (*ihr Was*).

Bultmann is suggesting that the Christ of the Fourth Gospel reveals not a " what " but a " who," not a truth about God, but God himself.

Though it is true that John is far more concerned with the " who " than with the " what " of the Gospel, he nevertheless recognizes that the revelation of a " who " implies the simultaneous revelation of a " what." To know a person, implies knowing *something* about that person. For John, the " who " and the " what " stand in paradoxical relation to each other.

As regards the " what-ness " of the revelation, John maintains that Jesus does reveal certain truths about himself, the world, man, and God: that God is a Spirit (ch. 4:24), that man must be born again of water and of the Spirit (ch. 3:5), that the " Comforter " will come (chs. 14:16, 26; 15:26; 16:7), that believing in him is necessary for eternal life (chs. 3:15; 20:31) that man and God are one (ch. 17), that love is the highest commandment (ch. 14), that he is the way, the truth, and the life (ch. 14:6), that God loves the world (ch. 3:16), et cetera. From John's standpoint, this is true knowledge and teaching of a sort, offered for the edification and increased self-understanding of the auditor.

However, in contrast with Matthew, who finds a whole
New Torah in Jesus, and contrary to Luke, who finds a philosophy of history revealed in Jesus and the Spirit, John offers comparably little in the way of concrete, easily memo-
rizable, " instant " teaching. John's chief purpose is to vivify
for his readers the " who " or the " thou " that Jesus reveals. We see this side of the picture in such passages as
these:

> If you had known me, you would have known my Father also;
> henceforth you know him and have seen him. (Ch. 14:7.) He who
> has seen me has seen the Father. (V. 9.) This is eternal life, that
> they know thee the only true God, and Jesus Christ whom thou
> hast sent. (Ch. 17:3.)

The knowledge or the " knowing " in these passages refers
to the knowledge of God, himself, not the knowledge of doctrine about God.

The venerable Greek term " glory " (*doxa*) plays a special role in John's revelation theology. Both in the Hellenistic
and Hebraic traditions, *doxa* (Hebrew, *cabhod*) can be defined as " the divine presence." When one speaks of beholding the " glory " of God, this means beholding a particular
self-manifestation of God. John says:

> And the word became flesh and dwelt among us, full of grace
> and truth; we have beheld his *glory* [*doxa*], *glory* as of the only
> Son from the Father. (Ch. 1:14.)

He means quite literally that Jesus reveals the presence of
God, or more precisely, that Jesus *is* the glory of God who
reveals this *doxa* in his miracles (ch. 2:11) and, above all,
in his crucifixion (ch. 12:16, 23).

The verb " glorify " (*doxazein*) also occupies a major position in John's working vocabulary. Because Jesus has " glorified," magnified, and declared the Father's presence in the
world, even now Jesus will be glorified:

Father, the hour has come; glorify thy Son that the Son may glorify thee. . . . And this is eternal life, that they know thee the only true God, and Jesus Christ whom thou hast sent. I glorified thee on the earth, having accomplished the work which thou gavest me to do; and now, Father, glorify thou me in thy own presence with the glory which I had with thee before the world was made. (Ch. 17:1, 3-5.)

The verb *doxazein* is employed with versatility by John to communicate the double thesis of his Gospel, that in Christ, God's presence is magnified; that because Christ has magnified God, he in turn has been magnified by God. In the language of paradoxical-mystical piety, John affirms both that God has revealed his Son and that the Son has revealed God. John sees in Christ the revelation of God, and in a sense he sees in this revelation of God a new revelation of the nature of Christ.

Christianity and Paradox

John's portrait of the " believer " manifests the same paradoxical-mystical brushstrokes found in his portrait of Jesus. With a typically dual approach to reality, John sets out to illumine three dimensions of Christian experience, the dimension of faith, of temporal existence, and of identity. He examines each with respect to its paradoxical character, pitting the concept of " trust " over against " belief," the concept of time over against eternity, and the concept of individuality over against community.

Faith and Paradox. The Fourth Gospel and the three Johannine letters are the only books in the New Testament in which the noun " faith " (Greek, *pistis*) does not appear. This deficiency, however, is more than compensated for by a superabundance of the verb " to believe " (Greek, *pisteuein*). This verb appears eleven times in Matthew, fifteen times in Mark, and nine in Luke, but makes *one hundred* appearances in John. Though the noun " faith " is totally lacking, the " faith concept " dominates the landscape.

Faith is two-dimensional in John. First, it is spoken of as synonymous with *belief*, " believing *that* " something is true about Jesus' identity, title, or pedigree. In deference to the needs of " belief," John develops an elaborate scheme of proofs often referred to as the Johannine theology of " signs." Jesus performs seven signs designed to prove his authority. The first occurs at the marriage feast in Cana (ch. 2:1-11); the second is the healing of the official's son (ch. 4:46-54); the third, the healing at the Pool of Bethesda (ch. 5:1-16); the fourth, the feeding of the five thousand (ch. 6:1-13); the fifth, Jesus' walking on water (vs. 14-21); the sixth, healing the man blind from his youth (ch. 9); and the seventh, raising Lazarus from the dead (ch. 11:1-46). Though commentators may argue over the precise number of signs, they agree that the " sign theology " is John's creation. Not only does he point an explicit finger at the first two " signs " (chs. 2:11; 4:54), he gives them special billing in his closing remarks:

Now Jesus did many other signs in the presence of the disciples, which are not written in this book; but these are written that you may believe that Jesus is the Christ, the Son of God, and that believing you may have life in his name. (Ch. 20:30-31.)

The function of " signs " is to justify *belief*.

The second dimension of the " faith concept " in the Fourth Gospel is its interpretation as " trust," with the emphasis on *believing in* rather than on *believing that*. The frequency with which the expression " believing in " occurs with verbs of " knowing " and " seeing " (Greek, *eidō, horaō, theōreō, ide*) suggests that " believing," " seeing," and " knowing " constitute one experience.

This paradoxical aspect of the " faith concept " in John, as a matter of belief, but also as a matter of perception, insight, trust, and revelation, appears quite pointedly in the dialogue that follows Jesus' healing of the man blind from birth:

> Jesus . . . said, " Do you believe in the Son of man? " He answered, " And who is he, sir, that I may believe in him? " Jesus said to him, " You have seen him, and it is he who speaks to you." He said, " Lord, I believe." (Ch. 9:35-38.)

The man's cry, " I believe," implies two affirmations: first, an existential perception and acceptance of Jesus as his Lord; second, an intellectual acceptance and belief that Jesus is the Son of Man. Both elements, the perceptive and the cognitive, constitute the Johannine concept of faith. Either is regarded as faith's legitimate starting point.

Temporal Existence and Paradox. The paradox of temporal existence originates in John's marriage of two concepts of time, the Hebraic and the Hellenistic. The Hebraic mind generally conceives of time as a linear process, leading from point x in the past to point y in the future. Evidence of the Hebraic time concept is found in John's reference to the period " before creation " when the Word was with God and was God (chs. 1:30; 8:58; 15:27; 17:5, 24), and to the period in the future when the judgment will take place (ch. 5:28-29).

A Hellenistic conception of time, or we might say, no-time, is equally present in John. For the Hellenist, ultimate reality, the realm of the ideas, was basically timeless. It was pure, windless, and removed from the jarring sounds of historical, material reality. We see traces of this empyrean thinking in the fact that John knows no real tragedy, no real suffering. The Passion narrative, far from being tragic, is an occasion for glory. Even Jesus, who is said to be true flesh, appears more as a spirit than a body. He is much less the long-awaited Hebraic Messiah than the Hellenistic emissary of light.

In reading this, the reader feels slightly schizophrenic. Should he orient his thinking upward to the eternal Ideas, or forward to the coming future judgment, " when the dead will hear the voice of the Son of God, and those who hear will live " (ch. 5:25)? John would propose that he look in both directions at once. This is possible, he would say, because in the Christ event, the past, the present, the future, and the eternal all telescope into one reality. This mystery and paradox is perhaps best seen in such passages as the following:

> Truly, truly, I say to you, *the hour is coming,* and *now is,* when the dead will hear the voice of the Son of God. . . . Do not marvel at this; for the hour is coming when all who are in the tombs will hear his voice and come forth, those who have done good, to the resurrection of life, and those who have done evil, to the resurrection of judgment. (Ch. 5:25, 28-29.)

Though we are told not to marvel at this, we cannot help puzzling over the perplexing paradox of the " coming hour " that " now is." On the one hand, the judgment, resurrection, eternal life, the Last Day, the era of " night," lie in the remote future (chs. 6:39-40, 44; 9:4; 11:9-10; 13:30, 36; 14:3; 16:32). But on the other, the resurrection has already taken place, the judgment has already occurred, eternal life is already available, and the era of " light " has already manifested itself (chs. 5:24; 3:18; 11:25-26; 8:51).

John holds tightly to both time and eternity. The Hebraist in him affirms the reality of history; the Hellenist in him affirms the reality of the timeless. The Hebraic strain maintains that the eternal is meaningless apart from the real flux and mutation in history; the Hellenistic asserts that the temporal is meaningless apart from the eternal ground of being in which the temporal is rooted. Continuity and discontinuity, fluctuation and change, stability and instability, are the polarities between which human existence transpires. Without the dedication to time, humanity, and history, life becomes irrelevant; without the commitment to eternity, life becomes rootless. For John, the Christ event illumines and embraces both realities, instructing man in the mysteries of the eternal as they relate to the redemption of the temporal.

Identity and Paradox. One of the key pieces of modern psychiatric hardware is the phrase " identity crisis." The psychotherapist uses this phrase to refer to the traumatic experience, characteristic of young adulthood, in which an individual finds himself confused over his identity or role in reality. In this context, the question, Who am I? is not the query of an amnesiac but the plea of a mind anxious over the meaning of his existence. How is he to think of himself? Primarily as a spirit or as a body? As a being of worth or as a cosmic cipher?

Christianity, in its perennial interest in the individual, has long taken the question of identity seriously. More recently, Paul Tillich, among others, has thrown some light on the problem by defining it in terms of the polarity between individuality and community, or to use his terms, " individuality and participation." For Tillich, a proper sense of identity depends on two mutually dependent experiences, the experience of authentic selfhood and the experience of authentic participation with an " other." The experience of participation is necessary for sharpening one's sense of individuality; and a proper sense of selfhood is the prerequisite for meaningful and communicative participation. If either is missing, identity becomes a problem.

John is concerned over individuality and community. Although he presupposes a sense of individuality in his readers, his purpose in writing is to show them how their individuality can be fulfilled by a mystical participation with Christ. The passage that follows is only one of many of its kind:

> Because I live, you will live also. In that day you will know that I am in my Father, and you in me, and I in you. (Ch. 14:19-20.)

The danger of this kind of language is that it is apt to encourage a kind of mystical disengagement from history. Even though John is basically a mystic in his orientation, he is nevertheless concerned with the necessity for historical responsibility (chs. 13:12-16; 15:13; 21:15-17).

Thus the problem John faces is to urge participation on two fronts: participation and community with God-in-Christ and participation and community with one's fellowman. Union with God is impossible without involvement in the needs of the world, and a fruitful union with man is impossible apart from the insight gained from communion with God. To express the paradox in prophetic terms, religion and ethics are inseparable.

John spells out the paradox in a string of key sayings. The first half of the paradox, union with God, is most graphically portrayed in the saying on the true vine:

> I am the true vine, and my Father is the vinedresser. . . . Abide in me, and I in you. As the branch cannot bear fruit by itself, unless it abides in the vine, neither can you, unless you abide in me. I am the vine, you are the branches. He who abides in me, and I in him, he it is that bears much fruit, for apart from me you can do nothing. (Ch. 15:1, 4-5.)

The second half of the paradox, the emphasis on human community, is expressed in the classic Johannine passage on the new commandment:

A new commandment I give to you, that you love one another; even as I have loved you, that you also love one another. By this all men will know that you are my disciples, if you have love for one another. . . . Greater love has no man than this, that a man lay down his life for his friends. (Chs. 13:34-35; 15:13.)

MYSTICISM, PARADOX, AND LOGOS

The battle between abstract and realistic art revives over the interpretation of the Fourth Gospel. To the literal-minded, the Fourth Gospel is pure, representational prose. But to those not committed to a literalistic interpretation, the Fourth Gospel is an example of impressionistic art— more precisely, theological poetry.

It has taken modern man some time to adjust to the non-representational intention in art, not to mention theology. Even such masters as Sir Thomas Beecham found it difficult to enjoy a piece of music without a melody. And the " realistic " school of painting still insists that a canvas must attempt the " most exact transcription possible " of life, as Edward Hopper, one of its representatives, has said. Yet there are many, perhaps the majority, who have negotiated the transition from representational to abstract art, having learned that even abstract art can have integrity if it gives full expression to the creative eye, ear, or hand of the composer as well as to the original vitality and life-burst of the subject portrayed. They have learned that both the artist and his subject will be the visible components in a finished work of art.

John is an artist. His Gospel reveals the image both of his genius and of the Logos that inspired this genius. Though some have called his interpretative, impressionistic method into question, there can be no doubt that it has legitimacy and integrity — as art, though certainly not as historical writing. John's symbolism and poetry are faithful to his vi-

sion. He is not describing the Logos as an " it," but as a vital
force in his own life. It is not a static charge isolated in time,
not even in the historical Jesus: " The *logos* which you hear
is not mine but the Father's who sent me " (ch. 14:24b); it
is a moving, inspiring spirit, operative from the beginning of
time (ch. 1:1), known to the prophets (chs. 1:35; 12:38),
and recently incarnated in Jesus of Nazareth (ch. 1:14). Its
activity does not stop, but in a sense begins anew there, as
it continues to appear in those disciples (ch. 8:31) who keep
and guard it (chs. 8:51-52, 55; 14:23; 15:20; 17:6), and
who, through their own *logos,* lead others to believe (ch.
17:20). In a paradoxical-mystical sense, John's Gospel itself
is Logos.

POSTSCRIPT

" But we have this treasure in earthen vessels . . ."
II Cor. 4:7.

THE EARTHEN CHARACTER of the Gospels is manifestly clear to a twentieth-century critical perspective. The succession of textual, source, and form critics has kept us conscious of the margin of creative distortion in the Gospels, that each of the writers has refracted the " good news " through the lens of his own disposition: Mark in existential seriousness, Matthew with apocalyptic urgency, Luke in panoramic joy, and John in beautiful but perplexing paradox.

The Gospel " treasure " that has been unearthed in the persistent digging of such critics as Luther, Wettstein, Baur, Bacon, Dibelius, Knox, and Bultmann is a rich lode. Its core is a legacy of " signs " and sayings that speak of " lostness " and " wholeness," guilt and forgiveness, death and rebirth. The intended audience is Everyman, the *am ha-aretz,* the man in the world.

The personal legacy from the four Evangelists is the physical, intellectual, and spiritual energy they invested in their Gospels. Their contributions are still visible, not only in the minutiae of editorialization, but most significantly in those sayings and stories that highlight their special interests:

121

MATTHEW   Every scribe who has been trained for the kingdom
          of heaven is like a householder who brings out of
          his treasure what is new and what is old. (Ch.
          13:52.)

MARK   Whoever would save his life will lose it; and who-
          ever loses his life for my sake and the gospel's will
          save it. (Ch. 8:35.)

LUKE   The Spirit of the Lord is upon me,
          because he has anointed me to preach
             good news to the poor.
          He has sent me to proclaim release to the captives
          and recovering of sight to the blind,
          to set at liberty those who are oppressed,
          to proclaim the acceptable year of the Lord.
                                              (Ch. 4:18-19.)

JOHN   In the beginning was the Word, and the Word was
          with God, and the Word was God. . . . In him was
          life, and the life was the light of men. The light
          shines in the darkness, and the darkness has not
          overcome it. (Ch. 1:1, 4-5.)

To understand this legacy demands dialogue with it, asking
questions, debating, and wrestling until it yields its blessing.

The word *kērygma,* proclamation, is a keynote of the Gospels. The Gospel writers insist that the Word must be pro-
claimed if it is to live in the world, and that such proclamation must be poured into " new wineskins " if it is to relate
to the plastic moods and tongues of the world. Paul shared
this belief in creating his letter to the Romans, often called
" the fifth Gospel," as did Augustine with *The City of God,*
Luther with his *Commentary on Romans,* Barth with *The
Word of God and the Word of Man,* H. Richard Niebuhr
with *The Meaning of Revelation,* and Paul Tillich with *The
Courage to Be.*

No one puts new wine into old wineskins; if he does, the wine
will burst the skins, and the wine is lost, and so are the skins; but
new wine is for fresh skins. (Mark 2:22.)

NOTES

1. Robert M. Grant, *The Secret Sayings of Jesus* (Dolphin Books, Doubleday and Company, Inc., 1960), pp. 146 and 151.

2. Burnet Hillman Streeter, *The Four Gospels* (The Macmillan Company, 1925), cf. pp. 150–154.

3. Burton Hamilton Throckmorton, ed., *Gospel Parallels: A Synopsis of the First Three Gospels* (Thomas Nelson & Sons, 1957).

4. Jean Wahl, *A Short History of Existentialism*, tr. by Forrest Williams and Stanley Maron (Philosophical Library, Inc., 1949), p. 1.

5. Calvin Schrag, *Existence and Freedom* (Northwestern University Press, 1961).

6. Søren Kierkegaard, *The Sickness Unto Death*, tr. by Walter Lowrie (Princeton University Press, 1951), p. 68; cited in Schrag, *op. cit.*, p. 4.

7. Wilhelm Wrede, *Das Messiasgeheimnis in den Evangelien* (Vandenhoeck & Ruprecht, Göttingen, 1901).

8. Sherman E. Johnson, *A Commentary on the Gospel According to St. Mark* (Black's New Testament Commentaries, Adam & Charles Black, Ltd., London, 1960), p. 9.

9. James Robinson, *The Problem of History in Mark* (Studies in Biblical Theology, No. 21, SCM Press Ltd., London, 1957), pp. 68–73.

10. Benjamin Bacon, *Studies in Matthew* (Henry Holt & Company, Inc., 1930), pp. 412 and 418.

11. Krister Stendahl, *The School of St. Matthew* (Acta Seminarii Neotestamentici Upsaliensis, XX, C. W. K. Gleerup, Lund, 1954), pp. 183 ff.

12. William H. Brownlee, " Biblical Interpretation Among the Sectaries of the Dead Sea Scrolls," *The Biblical Archaeologist*, XIV (1951), pp. 54–76; cited in Stendhal, *op. cit.*, pp. 184 ff.

13. Walter E. Bundy, *Jesus and the First Three Gospels* (Harvard University Press, 1955), pp. 93–94.

14. Edward P. Blair, *Jesus in the Gospel of Matthew* (Abingdon Press, 1960), p. 108.

15. R. H. Charles, tr., *The Testaments of the Twelve Patriarchs* (Adam & Charles Black, Ltd., London, 1908), p. 132.

16. Millar Burrows, *The Dead Sea Scrolls* (The Viking Press, Inc., 1955), p. 399.

17. Millar Burrows, *More Light on the Dead Sea Scrolls* (The Viking Press, Inc., 1958), pp. 285–286.

18. Martin Dibelius, " The Speeches in Acts and Ancient Historiography," *Studies in the Acts of the Apostles,* ed. by Heinrich Greeven; tr. by Mary Ling and Paul Schubert (Charles Scribner's Sons, 1956), p. 139.

19. Hans Conzelmann, *The Theology of St. Luke,* tr. by Geoffrey Buswell (Faber & Faber, Ltd., London, 1960).

20. Paul Schubert, " The Structure and Significance of Luke 24," *Neutestamentliche Studien für Rudolf Bultmann* (A. Töpelmann, Berlin, 1954), pp. 165–186.

21. Romano Guardini, " Dostoyevsky's Idiot, A Symbol of Christ? " tr. by Francis X. Quinn, *Cross Currents,* VI (1956), p. 368.

22. F. C. Grant, *Roman Hellenism and the New Testament* (Oliver & Boyd, Ltd., London, 1962), p. 105.

23. John A. T. Robinson, " The Destination and Purpose of St. John's Gospel," *Twelve New Testament Studies* (Studies in Biblical Theology, No. 34; SCM Press Ltd., London, 1962), pp. 107–125.

24. John Wright Buckham, " Mysticism," *Encyclopedia of Religion,* ed. by Vergilius Ferm (Philosophical Library, Inc., 1945), pp. 513–514.

25. Paul Tillich, *Systematic Theology* (The University of Chicago Press, 1957), II, pp. 83 and 86.

26. Rudolf Bultmann, *Theology of the New Testament,* tr. by Kendrick Grobel (Charles Scribner's Sons, 1955), II, p. 66.

INDEX

Acts, The, 78 f.

Am ha-aretz (people of the earth), 12, 121

Angels, 69 f.

Antiochus Epiphanes IV, 51

Apocalypticism, 49–54 *passim*, 61, 65, 99, 116

Apologetics, 13, 30, 84–88

Art: impressionistic, 119; of the Gospel writer, 19 f., 27, 38, 43, 97 ff., 105

Augustine, 103, 122

Bacon, B., 50, 62, 121

Barabbas, 42

Barth, K., 122

Beatitudes, 12, 73

Bethlehem, 18

Bethphage, 42

Biblical criticism. *See* Gospel criticism

Birth stories, 16, 18, 32, 60, 62, 74, 89

Blair, E., 60 f.

Bread, 37 f., 40 f., 62, 105, 108

Bread of Life. *See* Names and titles

Brooks, P., 60

Brownlee, W., 58

Buber, M., 24

Buckham, J. W., 103

Bultmann, R., 13, 103, 111, 121

Bundy, W., 61

Burrows, M., 70

Camus, A., 34 f.

Christ. *See* Names and titles

Christological question, the, 19 f., 29 f., 73 f., 90 f.

Church and community: conceptions of, 44 ff., 65–70, 74 f., 93–97, 117–119; functions of, 12, 14, 66

Comparative analysis of the Gospels, 20 ff.

Conzelmann, H., 82 ff.

Creation, 40, 77

Cursing the fig tree, 42

Daniel, 49, 51 f., 53

Dead Sea scrolls, 57, 69. *See also* Qumrân

Death, 26 f., 44, 106. *See also* Jesus: death of

Deuteronomy, 76

Diaspora, 84, 91, 101

Dibelius, M., 79, 121

Disciples, 43, 66

Docetics, 101

Dostoevsky, F., 98

Ecclesiastes, 76

Eckhardt, M., 103

Elijah, 28, 39

Emmanuel. *See* Names and titles

Emmaus, 16

Enoch, First, 52, 54

Ephesus, 13 f.

Esdras, Second, 52, 54

Essentialism, 26